KITES:
THE GENTLE ART OF HIGH FLYING

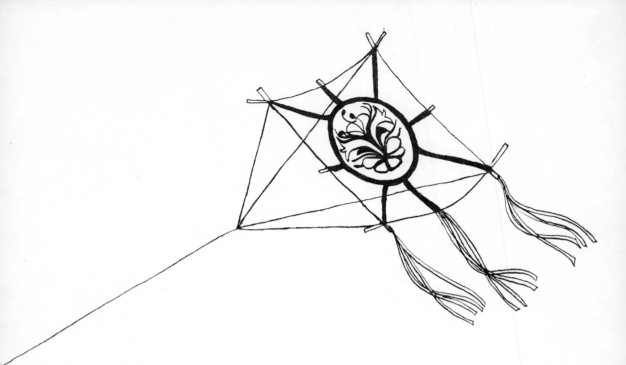

KITES:
THE GENTLE ART
OF HIGH FLYING

WRITTEN AND ILLUSTRATED BY
Susan Tyrrell

DOLPHIN BOOKS
Doubleday & Company, Inc., Garden City, New York   1978

A Dolphin Books Original
Doubleday & Company, Inc.

Library of Congress Cataloging in Publication Data

Tyrrell, Susan, 1952–
  Kites.

  Bibliography: p. 168.
  1. Kites. I. Title.
TL759.T95   629.133'32
ISBN 0-385-13055-4
Library of Congress Catalog Card Number 77–82774

For Richard, the rider of rainbows,
the wizard of winds.

ACKNOWLEDGMENTS

My special thanks to Lindy Hess; her constant enthusiasm and support were invaluable to this unseasoned author. And thanks, too, to Theodore T. Kuklinski, who lent me his private collection of kite books along with his notes from the MIT Kite Experimentation Laboratory. And, finally, special thanks to my husband, Richard Pastyrnak, for his creative criticism and love of kiteflying.

CONTENTS

FOREWORD

When the weather is warm and the wind is high, they appear—brightly colored pinions dancing toward the heavens. Kites have been around for thousands of years, but today America is in the midst of a kite renaissance.

Kite festivals are springing up throughout the country. An estimated 80 million kites are sold yearly in the United States, and the figures are on the rise. Kites have even entered college curricula: Massachusetts Institute of Technology recently founded a Kite Experimentation Laboratory after offering a successful course in kite making. Yale University has an official kiteflying team under the direction of famed kite master Will Yolen.

Why this sudden reinterest in kites? Some theorize that kites became more popular as the public lost interest in high-powered planes and space flight; people were still fascinated with flight, but preferred to observe the phenomenon on a more human scale. Others say it dovetails with the national concern for ecology— a kiteflier can spend a peaceful afternoon decorating the sky with fanciful shapes and colors while posing no threat to the environment.

Kiteflying is the ultimate high. It is an enjoyable way to escape our fast-paced lives and enter a state of total relaxation. Once you ride the wind on the end of a string you are never quite the same. It is a pleasant experience you will want to enjoy again and again, an experience no longer limited to children.

INTRODUCTION

From time to time, as I drive along the beaches near my home on Cape Cod, I'll glance toward the sky and catch a flicker of color dancing in the air. My eyes are drawn immediately back to the shore, searching out its master, wondering who it is and longing to participate in that momentary tug of war with the wind. Upon a closer examination of the scene, a child's silhouette suddenly appears. My first impulse is to rush home, grab my kites, and join my fellow flying enthusiast on the shore. And many times that is precisely what I have done.

When I began writing this book, my primary interest was to arouse and awaken those childhood kiteflying experiences present in almost all of us. I love kiteflying and I wanted to present the kite as a bridge back to those childhood dreams that have too often been buried beneath our adult inhibitions. Kites offer us a means to go back and recapture those times. A means to stimulate our senses and challenge a force greater than ourselves—the wind. Through kiteflying we can experience those private delights that are inexplainable to those who have not experienced them.

Who are these kitefliers, these lofters of painted colors that float on the edge of a breeze? In the past they have been dreamers, explorers, and inventors. Today the opportunity is open to everyone. Just try and catch the wind.

KITES:
THE GENTLE ART OF HIGH FLYING

KITE TALES

The art of kiteflying goes back at least two thousand years. It is believed that the first kite was flown long before the discovery of papyrus. Historians have had to depend on folklore to determine when and where the kite originated.

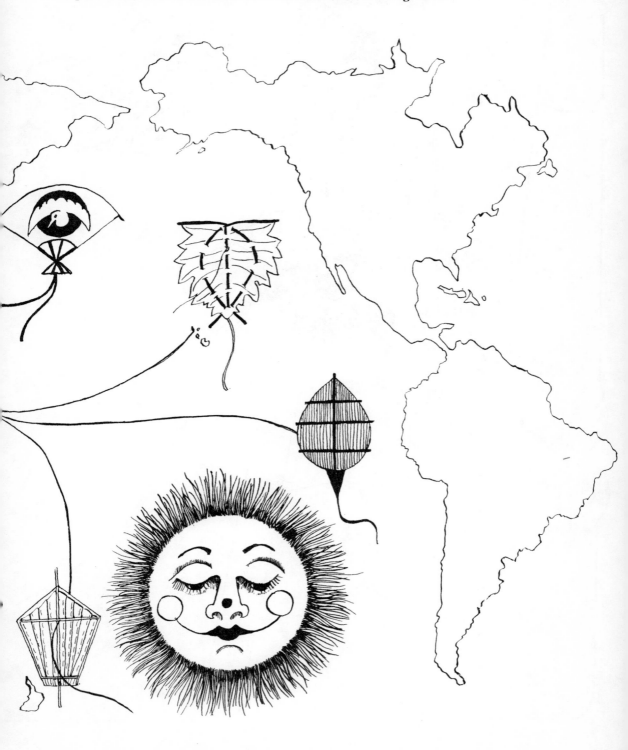

CHINA

The Chinese have been ingenious in their design and decoration of flat kites. Chinese history is filled with interesting tales and folklore based on kites flown for a serious purpose or for pleasure. Many tales have been woven around the first Chinese kite flight. One of the more colorful examples is the legendary story of the Emperor Shun.

The parents of the Emperor Shun were of a wicked nature. After many unsuccessful attempts to have the young Emperor killed, they ordered a granary built. When the boy was inside, the door was shut and bolted, and the building was set on fire. The young man fled to the top floor to escape the flames. The legend goes on to describe how a young child flew up to him a reed hat attached to a string. Shun sat on the hat and flew off to safety and freedom.

It is difficult to prove if the ride of Emperor Shun established the very first kite flight. Some historians believe the first kite to have been a banner or flag. Another theory of the origin of kites derives from an old method of hunting, when a string was attached to a hunter's arrow to prevent it from being lost in flight.

However it originated, the kite has enjoyed a long and interesting history. From China it flew and flourished in Korea, Japan, Polynesia, Egypt, and eventually around the world. It aided in many scientific discoveries and eventually led to the invention of the airplane.

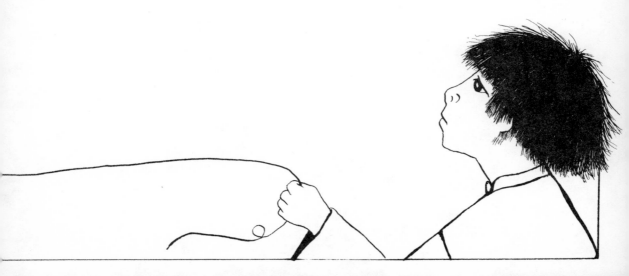

Another example of Chinese kite lore is the story of a famous general, Han Hsin. In the year 206 B.C. Han Hsin was commanding a rebel army that wanted to overthrow the tyrannical Emperor Wei Yang Kong. Because the insurgent army was small in number and ill-equipped in arms, a direct attack could prove disastrous. Their only chance to be successful would be through a surprise attack.

There seemed no way to infiltrate the palace for it lay in the midst of a vast plain. Any invasion could be seen easily for miles. Han therefore devised another way to gain entrance to the palace. He ordered his men to build a kite and sent it soaring into the heavens. When the kite flew directly over the palace, he marked and measured the string as the kite was pulled in. In this way he knew how long a tunnel would have to be that would bring his army well within the confines of the palace. In the dark of night the rebels worked to dig the tunnel. Upon its completion, the army crept into the unguarded courtyard. The attack proved victorious and General Han Hsin aided in establishing Liu Pang on the throne. This marked the beginning of the Western Han dynasty that was to rule the Chinese empire for two hundred years.

For centuries it has been traditional in China to fly kites on the ninth day of September. On this day each year the Chinese take to the hills for a day of picnicking and fun.

According to legend, the Festival of Ascending on High originated during the Sung dynasty (A.D. 960–1279). A farmer named Huan Ching was approached by a wise old seer, who warned him of an impending disaster. The seer informed the worried Ching that on the ninth day of the ninth month a calamity would befall his entire family. When the day of reckoning arrived, Ching decided to take his family into the hills for an outing. There they spent the day flying kites and drinking chrysanthemum wine.

In the evening when he and his family returned home, he found his house burned to cinders and all his livestock slaughtered. From that day on, each year, Ching and his family thanked the gods by declaring the ninth of September a holiday. The festival began to grow until it was declared a national holiday celebrated all over China by a giant kite festival.

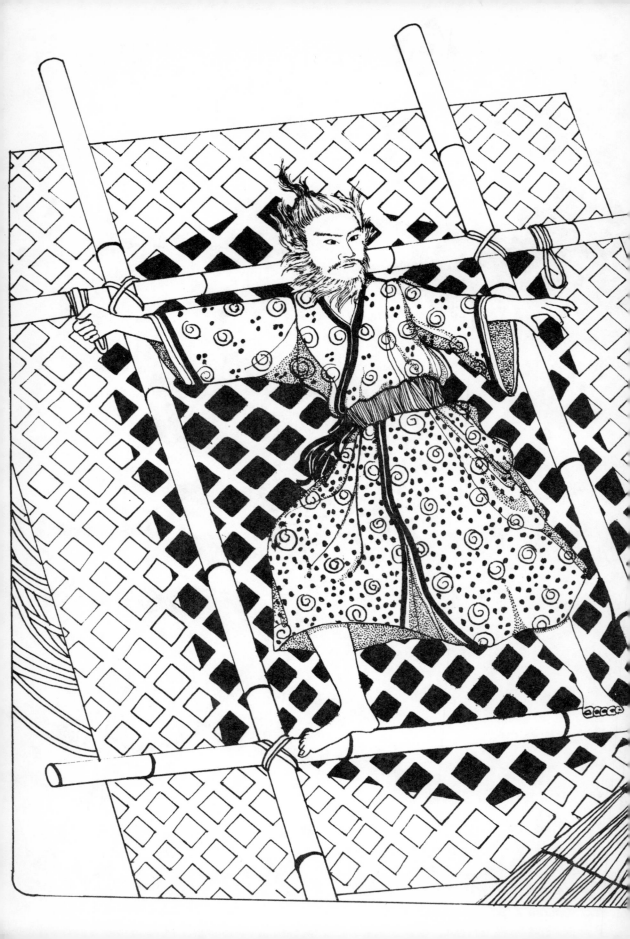

JAPAN

Although most experts contend that China is the birthplace of kites, other Eastern cultures have developed their own distinctive kite designs and kiteflying traditions.

In Japan kites were originally flown for religious purposes. The basic Chinese rectangular kite took on new forms in Japan. Cranes, turtles, and dragons could be seen flying in Japanese skies. Each design was symbolic—of long life, prosperity, fertility, and so on. Some kites brought good luck, while others frightened away evil spirits.

When a farmer's son comes of age in Japan, it is customary for him to be presented with a "rice kite," a special kite to fly over his own paddies. A sheaf of rice dangles from each side of the kite and one from the tail. When the kite is flown, the wind will shake loose the grains of rice and sow them over the ground. If the young farmer keeps his kite aloft until the last rice grain falls, it is a sign of prosperous harvests for the rest of his life.

Japanese legend tells of famed thief and folk hero Ishikawa Goyamen, who used a man-lifting kite in an attempt to steal the golden dolphins atop the Nagoya Temple. Fate, however, was not with him on that day. Although he landed safely on the roof and secured a few golden scales, he was caught and punished by being boiled in oil along with the rest of his family.

Another example of a man-lifting kite is described in this story of a famed samurai warrior: Minamoto No Tametomo, a warrior of the Genji clan, broke the law of the Emperor. He was punished by being exiled along with his son to the small island of Hachijo. Not wishing to have his son spend the rest of his life on a deserted island, Tametomo built a huge man-lifting kite. After tying his son to the kite, he was successful in lofting it back to the mainland. Consequently the now-famed Hachijo kite bears the portrait of Tametomo on its surface.

Much later a more practical application of kite lifting was found in Japan. It began when small objects were lifted into the air. Eventually supplies and tools were lofted in small baskets suspended from kites to aid workmen building towers.

Kiteflying is still a popular national pastime in modern-day Japan. On Boys' Day, May 5, the Japanese hold a tremendous kite festival. The tradition, dating back to 1550, is celebrated in every household that has been blessed with the birth of a boy within the last twelve months. Flags are flown bearing family crests and carp windsocks of various sizes and colors decorate the houses of those families with young boys under the age of seven.

The legend of the carp goes back thousands of years. In its journey up the treacherous streams of Japan, this hearty fish must fight swift river currents in its attempt to reach its spawning ground. The legend relates how a carp, after changing itself into a flying dragon, can ascend waterfalls and fly to its final destination; for this reason the carp is used to symbolize a boy's journey from adolescence to manhood.

General Yu Shin Kim.

KOREA

In Korea the new year begins with a family kiteflying festival. The name and birth date of each male child in a family is inscribed on the face of a separate kite. When the kite is soaring high in the heavens, the string is released. It is believed that the wind god will then blow the kite far away to distant lands and with it, any evil spirits that might affect the future prosperity of the child.

From the Silla dynasty, in the seventh century A.D., comes the tale of General Yu Shin Kim. According to the legend, rebellious subjects tried to overthrow Queen Jinduk. One moonless night, when the fighting was at its worst, a giant meteor fell to the earth. To the Queen's loyal troops, tired and disillusioned, this could only mean the fall of their beloved Queen. General Kim, realizing he would have to act fast in order to restore courage to the hearts of his men, built a giant kite and attached a lantern to its tail. That night as the troops slept, he lofted the kite into the black sky. As the kite ascended the general sent word to his men that the meteor was on the rise again. Believing this to be a favorable sign, the heartened troops went on to defeat the rebels, saving the Queen and her dynasty.

From Korea comes another colorful tale involving a clever general. In the twelfth century General Yong Cho was faced with an uncompromising dilemma. He had been sent by the Queen to a small island to put down a rebellion of her Mongolian subjects. Upon his arrival he found the villagers were based on steep cliffs above. In order to save the troops from defeat, he had his men build numerous kites. He lofted the kites from his invasion boats in the dead of night. To the kites were attached flaming torches. When the kites were well over the heads of the enemy he ordered the lines cut. This sent a shower of fire down upon the unsuspecting rebels. Although primitive in nature, this may have constituted the first air attack in history. The kite was no doubt introduced to the Korean people by Chinese Buddhist monks. Basic Korean kites were shaped similarly to the Chinese rectangle kite, with the exception of a circle cut out in the center. The kites are fast and graceful, able to hold their own in any kite fight.

POLYNESIA

It has been suggested that the kite was originally introduced to the Pacific islands by Christian missionaries. Ironically, they were used in many pagan rites; kites were believed to be a means of communicating with the gods. There are many stories concerning these celestial communications. Perhaps the most popular is the tale of the wind gods.

The twin wind gods Rongo and Tane were avid kitefliers. In one ritual, Tane challenged Rongo to a kite contest. Rongo, who was wiser than his brother, secretly attached an enormously long string to his kite. Naturally he won the contest. For this reason, the first kite up during any kite festival is always named for Rongo and dedicated to him.

Another tale frequently told is the story of an unhappy mother who discovered her two young sons missing. The woman, frantic with worry, consulted a priest to help her in finding her sons. The priest used two kites to discover the whereabouts of the missing boys. He named a kite for each of the boys and sent them soaring into the sky. The kites rose steadily and then hovered over the hut of an old chief. It later became clear that the chief had murdered the boys and he was severely punished.

EGYPT

Though China is generally given credit for being the place where kites originated, some evidence as ancient as that of China has been found in Egypt. Hieroglyphics carved in stone and drawn on papyrus show early that kites existed there as well. A papyrus from Elephantine Island, in the Nile, dating back to 500 B.C., relates this story of a jealous Pharaoh.

According to the hieroglyphics, the Pharaoh was trying to discredit a clever vizier named Ahikar. Ahikar was very popular with the common people. This bothered the Pharaoh and threatened his place of importance with his followers. In order to rid himself of the vizier, the Pharaoh ordered him to build a palace midway between heaven and earth. If he failed to do so, death would be his punishment. Ahikar built two kites in the shape of eagles. He sent two boys to mount the kites and lofted the kites one hundred feet into the air. They looked indeed as though they were between heaven and earth. As the vizier instructed, the boys called down to the Pharaoh and asked him to fly up with the necessary materials. The Pharaoh was a god and according to the prophets, all gods could fly. Rather than discredit himself the Pharaoh abandoned the idea and ordered the project stopped. Through his cleverness Ahikar was able to save his life and enhance his reputation.

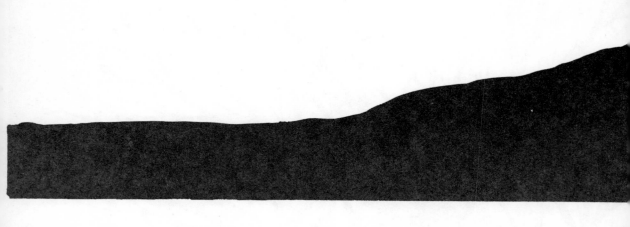

Though it is possible that kites were invented independently in different parts of the world, it is more likely that they were spread through trading among the various cultures. That would account for the existence of the same kite forms that we have evidence of in ancient times in various places in the eastern hemisphere.

Kites were introduced to the Western world around 400 B.C. A Greek scientist named Archytas, in the fourth century B.C., was said to have flown a wooden bird-shaped kite over the ancient colonial port of Tarentum (modern Taranto). There has been some speculation by historians as to whether the bird was indeed a kite. It seems that many early civilizations used the words "kite" and "bird" interchangeably, thus making clear evidence of early kiteflying difficult to point to.

Marco Polo is thought to have brought the kite back to the West in A.D. 1295 after his expedition to China. However, a kite is only mentioned once, briefly, in Polo's manuscripts. After his death, the kite, in the form of windsocks, became popular among Christian leaders in Europe, who used it to simulate godlike apparitions.

In the East, the kite developed and flourished, and as it moved West many changes occurred. The delicate construction and symbolic decorations disappeared. The kite slowly evolved into an instrument of science and experimentation.

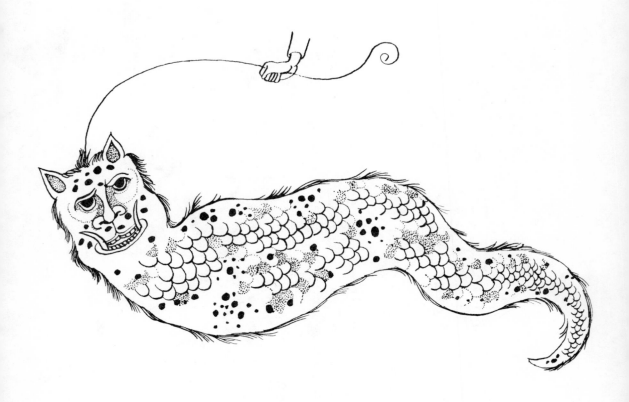

MAN, DREAMS, AND FLYING MACHINES

Kites have lifted men into the air, towed carriages across the countryside, frightened armies into retreat, aided in sending the first message across the Atlantic, assisted in forecasting the weather, and explained some of the mysteries of electricity.

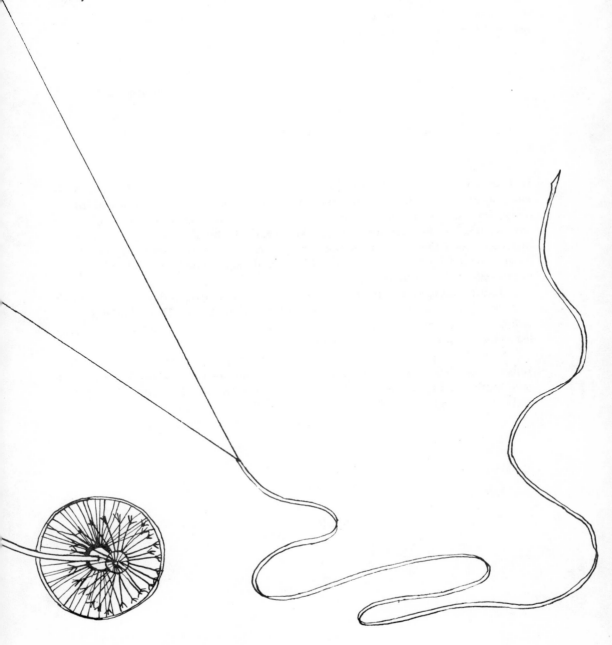

The first documented kite experiment in Europe took place in Scotland in 1749—thirty years before the first balloon flight and about one hundred and fifty years before the invention of the airplane.

WILSON AND MELVILLE

In Glasgow, two young Scottish scientists, Alexander Wilson and Thomas Melville, decided to explore the temperature of the atmosphere at various altitudes. They flew six paper kites in tandem, with a thermometer attached to each. At varying heights the thermometers, packed neatly in bundles of paper to prevent breakage when they landed on the earth, were released by means of time fuses. After several trials, Wilson and Melville proved their hypothesis that colder temperatures did exist at higher altitudes.

Because they were only students at the time of their experiments, their thesis on atmospheric temperature went unnoticed until 1825. Their findings were brought to the public's attention when the notes on their experiments were published along with Dr. Wilson's memoirs.

Kites have played a major part in meteorological studies for many years. Wilson and Melville helped to pioneer the way for such important figures in science as Benjamin Franklin, Guglielmo Marconi, Lawrence Hargrave, and Wilbur and Orville Wright.

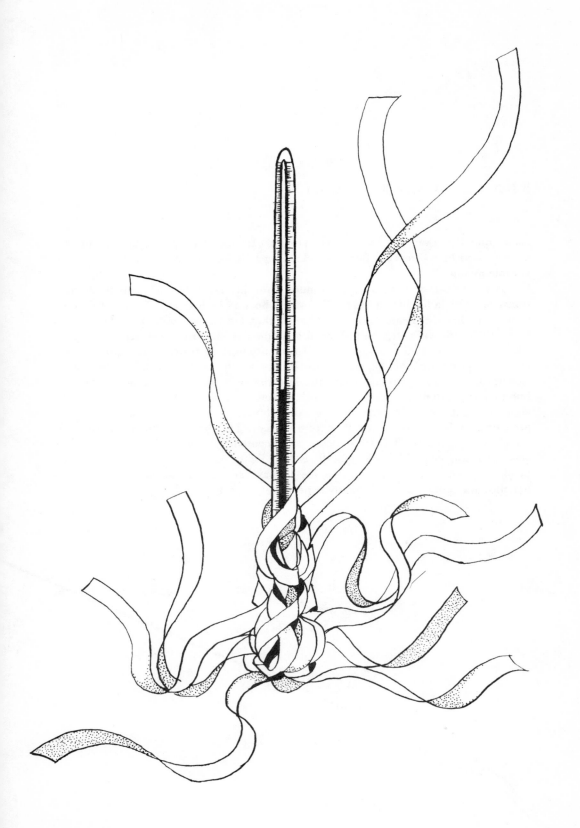

BENJAMIN FRANKLIN

As a child Ben Franklin was an avid kiteflier. In one of his youthful experiments, a kite towed him across his favorite swimming hole in what he termed "a most favorable manner."

His fascination with kites continued into his later life. During a thunder storm near Philadelphia in July 1752, when he was in his early forties, Franklin, along with his son, headed for an old shed that lay in the midst of a large open field. With little difficulty, he fashioned a simple flat kite from two slender strips of cedar and his own silk handkerchief. In an attempt to prove that lightning had electrical properties, he lofted the small kite at the end of a thin wire into a stormy sky. As the lightning struck the kite the electricity traveled down the wire line to a key fastened to its end by a silk ribbon. Franklin took care to stand in the doorway of the shed in order to keep the ribbon dry. When the rain thoroughly drenched the kite, fiery streaks flew from the key. The dry silk ribbon was the only thing that prevented Ben from being electrocuted. Although Benjamin Franklin was successful in proving his hypothesis that lightning was electricity, unbeknown to him a Frenchman by the named De Romas had had the same hypothesis earlier, but was only successful in his experiment a year after Franklin.

GEORGE POCOCK

Seventy-five years after Franklin's experiments in Philadelphia, an English school-master began experimenting with the lifting and pulling properties of the kite.

In Bristol, England, in 1825, George Pocock became obsessed with the idea that kites could be used to pull various objects from one place to another. After many designs and much preparation he was able to prove his conjectures with the invention of his "charvolant" (kite carriage). Drawn by two specially designed flat kites, flown in train, the carriage successfully towed a group of four people across the countryside, at the speed of twenty-five miles per hour.

Pocock also believed that kites could be used to aid shipwrecked sailors. To prove his point, he used a kite to lift his son from a beach to a nearby cliff while seated in an armchair suspended from heavy wire. After alighting on the cliff top, the boy returned to the chair, released the necessary lines, and slid down the tow-line in his chair to his father back on beach. Luckily the boy's weight caused the towline to belly, which slowed down the chair so that he landed safely.

Through other experiments with kites, Pocock was the first to discover that the wind is stronger at higher altitudes. This became invaluable information to those experimenters who were to follow.

BADEN FLETCHER SMYTH BADEN-POWELL

In 1894, a captain in the Scots Guards, B. F. S. Baden-Powell, developed a way of putting kites to use for military purpose. An avid balloonist, he designed and built six hexagonal kites based on the Rokkaku kite native to Japan. He flew them in tandem and was successful in lifting a man into the air. The stability of the kites was increased when they were flown on a series of twin lines. In 1895 he patented his design after experimenting with various materials and sizes. Army officials were so enthusiastic about his experiments that they incorporated the idea and used kites to lift fully equipped aerial observers during the Boer War (1899–1902). Baden-Powell was convinced that kites could also be used as effectively to relay messages and to signal troops in remote areas. His "levitor kite," as he called it, was also used to lift cameras into the air. This was believed to be the first attempt at aerial photography.

WILLIAM A. EDDY

Eddy, an American meteorologist, started out as a journalist in Bayonne, New Jersey. In 1894, dropping journalism, he became a full-time inventor and designed a kite that helped revolutionize the development of meteorological study in the Western world. Eddy found out that by bowing the center kite spar and using a loose-fitting cover he could achieve greater lift and eliminate the kite tail. In 1894, he introduced his design to the U. S. Weather Bureau Blue Hills Observatory, south of Boston. After extensive investigation the Bureau found the Eddy kite stable enough to lift heavy instruments to altitudes of from one thousand to fifteen thousand feet. Eddy's kite made it possible for weather observers to record information previously inaccessible to man.

A few years after the first experiments with kite photography in England, Eddy became the first American to test his own theories on the subject. Opposed to the use of time fuses to release a camera's shutter, he devised a way to use strings controlled from the ground to achieve the same results. At one point in his experimentation he fastened eight cameras to a round platform and lofted them high into the air. With the cameras all pointing in different directions he was able to take eight pictures simultaneously, thus obtaining a circular picture of the horizon.

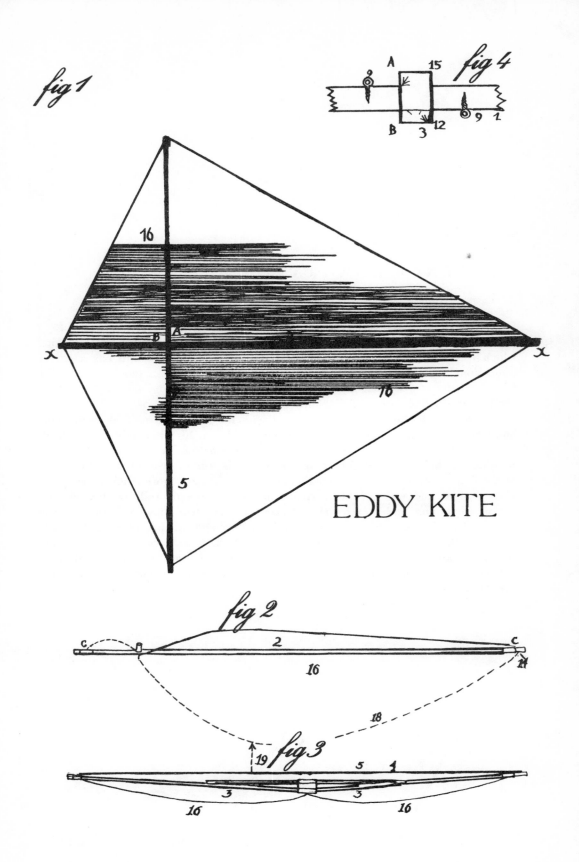

fig 1

fig 4

EDDY KITE

fig 2

fig 3

LAWRENCE HARGRAVE

In the 1890s a British-born Australian named Lawrence Hargrave took Eddy's experiments with a bowed kite one step further when he invented the box kite, which was also used by the U. S. Weather Bureau. The box kite has a three-dimensional cellular design with a rigid structure, making it a much more stable kite than any of its predecessors. The box kite turned out to be the immediate forebear of the first successful airplane.

In his youth Hargrave was fascinated with the idea of flying and spent many hours studying birds careening through the sky. Upon his discovery of how birds are able to soar without the flapping movement of their wings, Hargrave refashioned the kite world. The main result of his studies evolved into the design of the first non-flat kite. His three-dimensional kite proved more efficient than previous designs and was capable of maintaining its strength and stability in very strong winds and under extremely adverse weather conditions. Although he was successful at the early stages of manned-flight development, his ultimate dream of designing the first flying machine was never realized. A true scientist, he chose not to patent his box-kite invention. He believed his designs and accomplishments belonged to all men and should be readily available to anyone who could put them to good use.

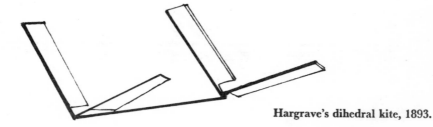

Hargrave's dihedral kite, 1893.

Hargrave's unsuccessful design for a flying machine.

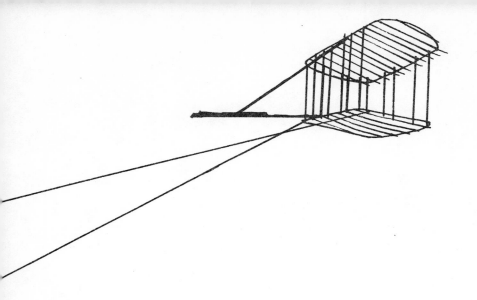

THE WRIGHT BROTHERS

In Kitty Hawk, North Carolina, on the Atlantic Ocean, two brothers, Wilbur and Orville Wright, spent many hours studying and flying the Hargrave box kite. They built numerous wind tunnels and experimented with the shapes of kites in relation to their lifting properties. After some minor adjustments in design, they flew their first glider as a kite to test its stability in the air. The glider was·controlled from the ground and during appropriate weather conditions manned and controlled from the glider itself. On December 17, 1903, with the addition of a gasoline-powered engine and a propeller, the kite became the first successful man-carrying airplane. It wasn't long before the plane replaced the kite for military observation as well as for weather study.

Today airplanes can travel faster than the speed of sound and advanced aeronautics, in 1968, placed man on the moon. Their very first flight seventy-five years ago was roughly half the length of the wingspan of a modern Boeing 747.

LEONARDO DA VINCI

Many inventors have experimented with kites at one time or another. In the fifteenth century Leonardo da Vinci, for example, devised a method of spanning vast rivers and gorges with the help of kites. His method was employed much later when a kite was used to carry a cable across the Niagara Gorge, in the 1850s, to enable one of the first great suspension bridges to be built. (It survived for forty-two years.)

During his kite experiments, Da Vinci became obsessed with the idea of artificial flight. He labored for twenty-five years on a design for a flying machine. Unfortunately, he believed all his designs to be clumsy and superfluous, since his efforts—to simulate birds in flight—ended unsuccessfully.

Sometimes his obsession with manned flight resulted in strange inventions, such as a very impractical pair of mechanical wings. Most likely, it was his interest with kites that led him to study cloud formations and air currents. These studies in turn led to his invention of a pyramidal parachute, the earliest known evidence of any such device. Scientists are still interested in his design for a helical airscrew. It is regarded today by aeronautical engineers to be the predecessor to the helicopter, but Da Vinci considered his device to be a minor accomplishment because it was derived from a child's toy.

Da Vinci's obsession with kites led him to design strange devices.

Above: Helical airscrew. Far right: Study of cloud movements and patterns. Right: Pyramidal parachute.

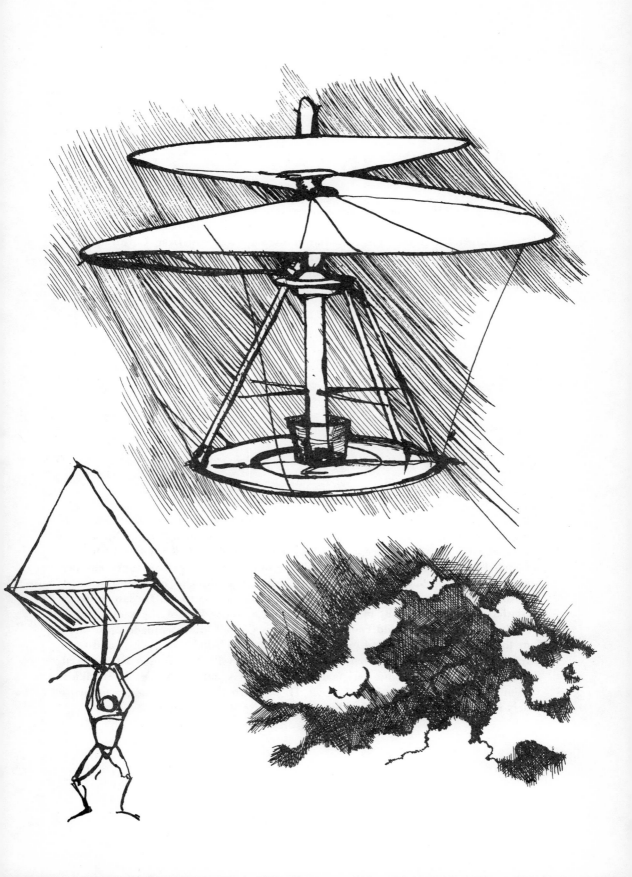

GUGLIELMO MARCONI

In December 1901, at the age of twenty-seven, Guglielmo Marconi in St. John's, Newfoundland, used a kite to loft a radio antenna four hundred feet into the air. A few moments later the first transatlantic message was sent from Cornwall, England, and received by Marconi in Newfoundland. Since that time kites capable of lofting radio antennae have been considered standard communication equipment in life rafts of many air forces, including that of the United States.

ALEXANDER GRAHAM BELL

Alexander Graham Bell, the inventor of the telephone, also experimented with kites; he was interested in the new rigid designs. In the early 1900s, in Nova Scotia, he expanded on the concept and designed a kite shaped like a tetrahedron, a four-sided solid with triangular faces. His tetrahedron consisted of four cells per unit. To allow for dihedral lift, he only covered two sides of each unit surface. Bell found that a medium wind was required to lift a small kite. He later discovered that the same amount of wind would lift a larger kite of the same design. Bell then proceeded to build enormous kites; his Cygnet kite was made up of over four thousand cells. He needed only a slightly stronger wind to launch it and once lifted a man nearly two hundred feet into the air. In 1907 he founded the Aerial Experiment Association and designed the famous Cygnet II. A slightly modified version of its predecessor, the Cygnet II was fitted with an engine; unfortunately it did not generate sufficient lift to get the kite off the ground.

An adaptation of a self-promotional poster featuring Samuel Cody and his famed war kite.

SAMUEL FRANKLIN CODY

Around the time of Bell's experimentation with mammoth kites in Canada, the Texas-born Colonel Samuel F. Cody was doing some independent work with kites in England, of which he was a naturalized citizen. Not as well known as his good friend and look-alike William F. Cody—famed as Buffalo Bill—Sam Cody, who liked to dress like Buffalo Bill, also had a colorful past behind him and searched for something to fill his emotional need for excitement. Like the kite pioneers before him, he began testing by flying kites in tandem. It wasn't long before Cody added wings to the Hargrave box-kite design and began exploring the possibility of using kites for towing. Successful in his early kite ventures, in 1901 he towed a small dinghy across the English Channel in just under thirteen hours. Cody went on from flying kites to become the first man in England to fly an airplane. In 1908, after months of diligent work, Cody presented his "Flying Cathedral" to the world. The largest plane built at that time, it broke all previous records when it flew forty miles across the English countryside. His experiments continued until 1913, when while flying his latest creation, the Waterplane, the craft broke apart in mid-air, killing Cody and a passenger over Laffans Plain, near Farnborough. This constituted one of the earliest fatalities in air history.

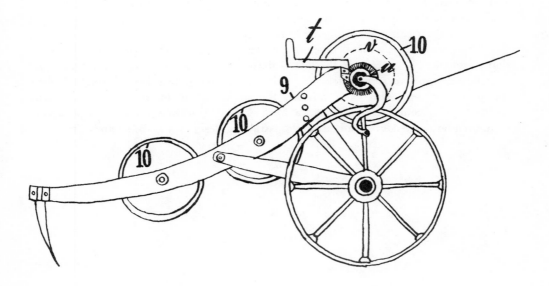

Patent drawing for Cody's winch with interchangeable drums.

After so many years of productive experiments. It is hard to understand why the kite was virtually forgotten by science in the early twentieth century. For thirty years it lay neglected, reduced to nothing more than a child's toy. It wasn't until the design of the new "soft kites" in the 1940s that America found itself in the midst of a kite renaissance.

FRANCIS M. ROGALLO

An aeronautical engineer later with the United States National Aeronautics and Space Administration (NASA), Francis Rogallo designed the first nonrigid kite, the "parawing," in 1943. He believed that a kite should conform to the wind—not the other way around. The space program became interested in his concept and involved Rogallo in extensive research, testing his designs in high-powered wind tunnels. The space program hoped the parawing would aid in landing space capsules safely within their designated target areas.

The parawing is a flexible, cloth or plastic square with a parachutelike tension structure. The surface of the kite is shaped by the push of the wind against it. Rogallo's design had some interesting spin-offs. Hang gliders were developed from the parawing and with their advent, the dream of many great inventors was realized—man could now soar like a bird. A few American aircraft corporations have even been considering adapting the parawing design for manned aircraft.

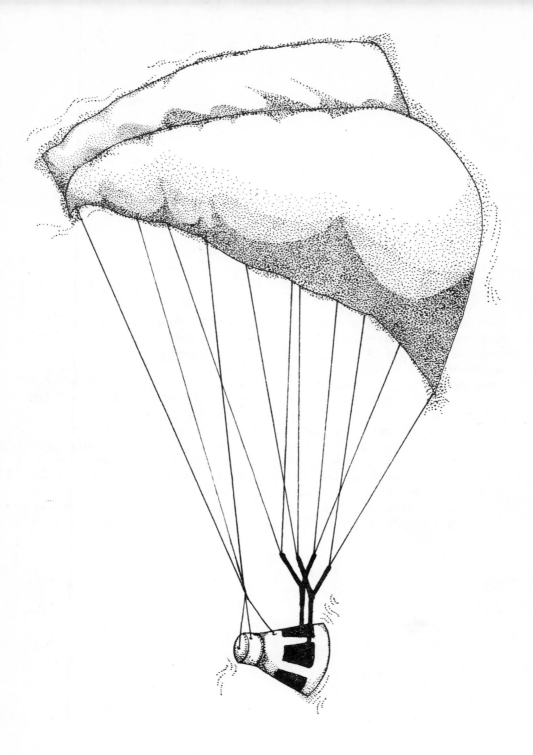

Rogallo's parawing during tests for a new space capsule re-entry project.

DOMINA JALBERT

The "parafoil" is one of the most interesting recent developments in the kiteflying world. In the 1960s Domina Jalbert, an American aeronautical engineer, decided to harness the energy of the wind. Jalbert first measured the cross section of an airplane wing, then used those basic measurements to design a multicelled kite joined together only with fabric. This nonrigid kite was designed to let the wind give it its shape. The kite is similar to a windsock, but it is closed at one end. Jalbert attached several keels, or vanes, beneath his parafoil and added a multi-stringed bridle. His theory was that as the kite was held up facing into the wind, the air would fill the compartments, transforming the kite into an airfoil. Lift would be provided by air flowing under and over the inflated parafoil. The air-borne kite looks like a multicolored pillow in the sky. With the design of the parafoil in 1964, the kite world was given it strongest lifter. When one flies a large version of the kite, a weight test is needed and the towline should be tied securely to a power winch, car, or tree to prevent its flier from involuntarily taking off too.

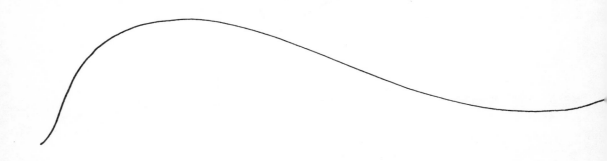

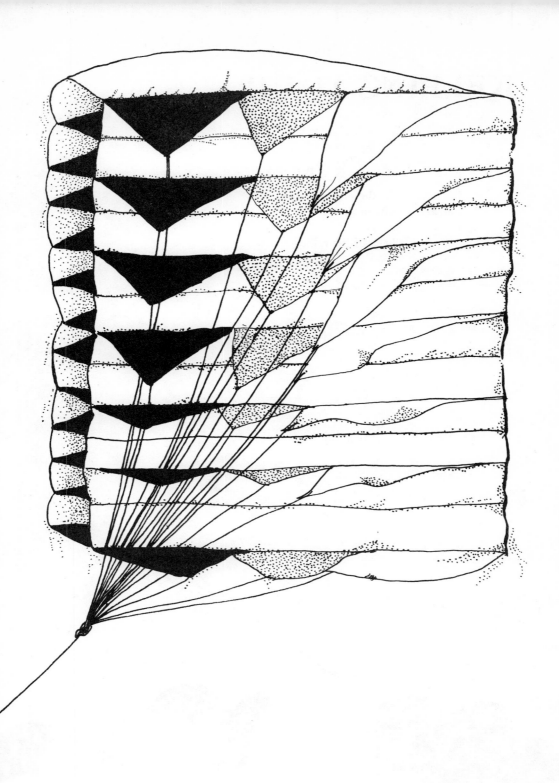

KEEPING IT UP

FLYING A KITE

My kite is like the morning star,
an early candle in the sun,
my kite is beauty
    on the back of the rolling wind.

King Gupta

WHAT IS A KITE?

Kites have existed for thousands of years; in their earliest form they took the shape of large leaves flown from twisted vines. However, only since the nineteenth century have we been able to determine just what a kite is and why it flies.

In the early 1800s a British scientist, Sir George Cayley, began an intense study of birds in flight. After many months of observation he was able to determine that the angle at which a bird moves his wings through the air determines the bird's upward movement. From Cayley's observations we are able to ascertain that a kite is a surface shaped to be lifted by a breeze. To keep the kite from being carried away, a line held by the flier is attached to it to keep it steady while the air rushes past it. In contrast to the motion of the bird, which moves forward through the air by itself, the kite is held more or less in the same place, while the air is allowed to send it higher and higher toward heaven.

Cayley's design for a man-carrying glider, 1852.

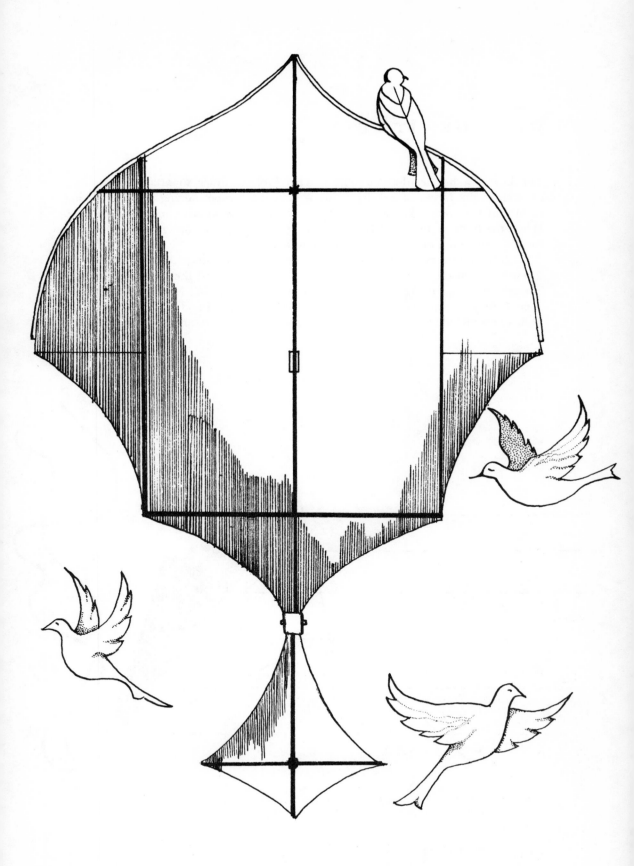

WHY DOES IT FLY?

The kite is a heavier-than-air object. Therefore, in order to attain lift it must counteract the forces of gravity. This is achieved by positioning the kite's wing surface at the appropriate angle to the direction of the wind by means of a bridle. When the force of the wind is strong enough to overpower the gravitational pull, the kite can obtain lift from it and rise up into the air.

"Lift" refers to the forces that enable the kite to defy the law of gravity. These forces in the case of a kite are actually the wind and the effect a particular kite design has on it. Another basic fundamental of kiteflying is "drag." Drag consists of the basic factors of kite design that resist the wind and create a downward pull. These include the kite's shape, weight, and surface covering.

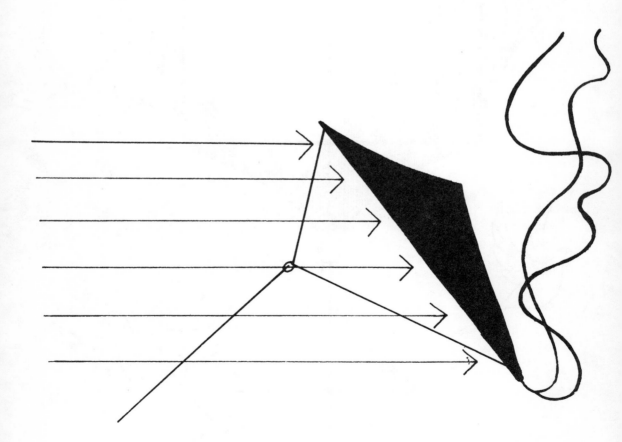

Diamond kite at a high angle of attack.

The ratio between lift and drag in a kite determines how well a particular design will fly. For example, if there is a minimum of drag in relation to the lift it will result in a high-flying angle—the kite will achieve height as well as distance. If the drag is at a maximum, the kite will have a low angle of attack into the wind—the kite will fly flat out as opposed to up and out. Should the amount of drag be substantially greater than the amount of lift, the kite will never rise up off the ground.

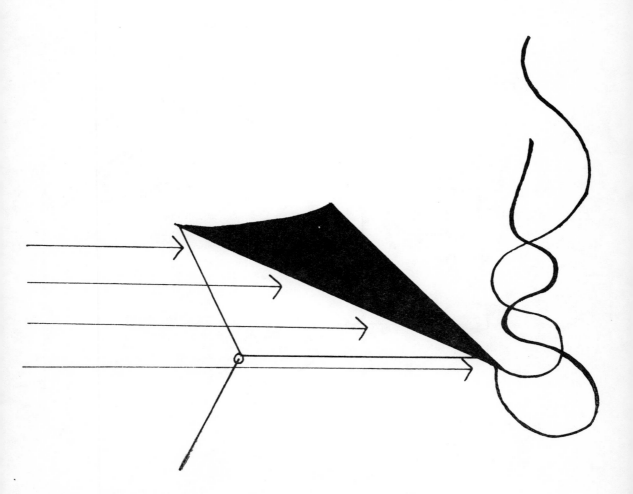

The same diamond kite, with a slight bridle adjustment, at a low angle of attack.

BRIDLES

The bridle is the string or strings attaching the flying line to the kite. The bridle and its points of connection are critical to the kite's performance. The basic two-legged bridle is attached on one end about one third of the way down from the top of the kite and the other end to the kite's base. To insure equal distribution of the wind upon the kite's surface the bridle can be adjusted, in order to assure the kite's stability by maintaining an effective angle of attack.

The length of the bridle will vary depending on the size of the kite. It is standard to use line approximately four times the length between the two connection points. The next step is attaching the flying line to the proper point on the bridle, commonly referred to as the "tow point."

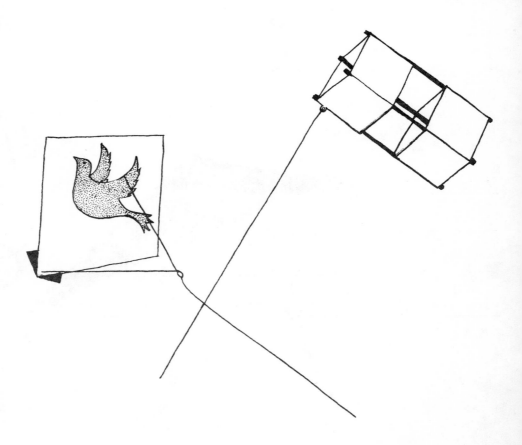

The Hargrave box kite is the only kite that can be flown successfully with the flying line connected directly to its flying surface. Most other kite designs require at least a two-legged bridle. There are no steadfast rules governing the number of legs, or shrouds, a bridle must have. The basic size and shape of the kite will determine how it will be bridled. It could have just two legs or have hundreds of legs, as in the case of the famed Japanese Hoshubana kites (the Hoshubana kites are forty-eight by thirty-six feet, with bridle lines that average a hundred feet in length).

When adjusting the bridle it is important to remember that a high angle of attack is required for low-speed winds and a low angle is required for high-speed winds. This basic information will help the kiteflier to have more control.

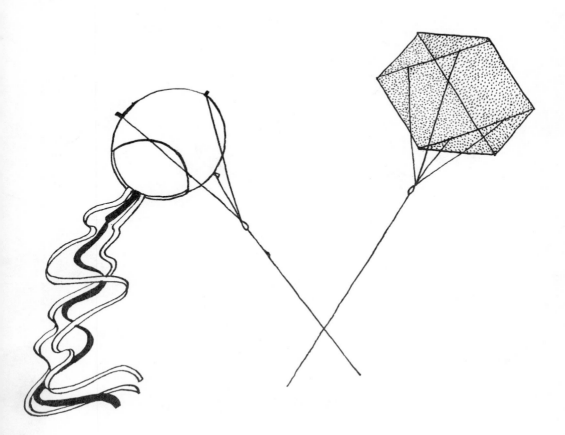

An adaptation of a fifteenth-century draco, or drogue.

TAILS, DROGUES, AND WINDSOCKS

A tail is designed to stabilize a kite and hold it facing into the wind by producing drag. Drag should not be confused with weight. When one is designing a tail, it is important to remember that it is its length and not its weight that helps to stabilize the kite. The average tail should be at least five times the entire length of the kite. However, the length may vary for different wind conditions.

Although the flat kite is dependent on its tail for drag, other kite designs with built-in stability can benefit from a tail's extra stabilizing effect in strong winds. Kites normally classified as light-wind fliers increase their flying capabilities with the use of a tail.

The drogue, which is another type of stabilizer, was invented by Sir George Nares in the nineteenth century. Although it works in much the same way as a tail, the drogue has the advantage of being self-regulating. Because it is basically the frustum of a cone, open at both ends, the drogue takes in more air than it lets out, which allows it to regulate the amount of air it expels. It is particularly effective in producing extra drag in a heavy, pulling kite such as the parafoil.

A windsock is a cloth bag the same shape as a drogue and open at both ends. It is attached to the top of a pole and used to indicate the direction of the wind by the current of air that blows through it. Most prominent at small airports, windsocks can produce drag for kites when they are used as drogues. Colorful carp windsocks from Japan can also be flown off a kite's towing line as an extra source of amusement for the kiteflier.

L I N E

Line can be string, button thread, or fishing line; it can be made of cotton, hemp, or twisted or braided nylon. The type of line most suitable for each kite depends on the amount of pull needed to loft a particular design. A cloth kite, for example, would require a much stronger line than a paper or plastic kite.

The kite line available in most drugstores and department stores is usually cotton line, about ten-pound breaking strength (called "test"). Cotton line is fine for paper or light plastic kites, but don't try to fly a cloth kite from it unless you are prepared to lose the kite. When choosing line, it is essential for you to realize that the line itself is capable of producing its own drag. Therefore, the weight of the line can prove a critical factor. In order to avoid unwanted drag, the lightest and strongest line should be used.

Monofilament line is extremely light for its strength. It is also readily available to most kitefliers. However, there are two important points that must be considered before you decide to use it. First, monofilament line has a tendency to stretch under excessive pulling. This would eventually cause stress points in the line, where it could break. Second, it can cut your hands when you are kiteflying; for this reason always wear gloves when you use it.

Twisted nylon line is made up of three separate strands twisted together. Although it is light and relatively strong, the individual strands have been known to separate while the kite is being flown. However, this can sometimes be helpful because it gives the line more elasticity. But when it is time to reel the kite in, the untwisted line has a tendency to tangle and knot up, to the point of being unusable.

The more popular braided nylon line is available in test strengths of ten, twenty, thirty, fifty, eighty, and one hundred pounds. Light in weight but very strong, this line can be found in kite shops and sporting-goods stores, at no great expense to the kiteflier. Braided line is easy to use and it doesn't twist or knot under pressure.

Most kites come with instructions listing the types and test strengths of line required. If you are building your own kite, simply measure the surface of the kite in square feet and multiply that number by three; this should give you the correct number of pounds test strength your kite will need.

WIND

It is a popular misconception that a kite needs a tremendous blast of wind to get off the ground. The most successful kiteflying is done in the winds from four to twenty miles per hour. Although the winds at ground level may be relatively light, it is important to remember the findings of George Pocock in 1825, when he discovered that stronger winds existed at higher altitudes.

Wind is air in motion caused by uneven atmospheric temperatures, which in turn cause differences in pressure. Wind is formed when these imbalances strive to regain balance. This helps to explain why in early spring, when there is a vast difference in the temperature between the equator and the north polar regions, March "comes in like a lion and goes out like a lamb."

In 1805 Rear Admiral Sir Francis Beaufort of the Royal Navy devised a twelve-point wind scale to aid sailors at sea, with 0 rated as a dead calm and 12 as a hurricane. Scale numbers 1 to 6 are appropriate for kiteflying.

THE BEAUFORT SCALE

Scale	Wind Speed			Types of Kites
1	1–3	mph	smoke drifts lazily	paper
2	4–7	mph	tree leaves rustle	paper and light plastic
3	8–12	mph	small flags fly and leaves dance	plastic
4	13–18	mph	trees toss, dust flies	plastic, light cloth
5	19–24	mph	small trees sway	cloth
6	25–31	mph	kiteflying is risky	large, cloth

Here is a simple test that will tell you if there is enough wind for your particular kite. With your back to the wind, hold the kite up by its bridle. If the kite assumes flying position conditions are good. When your kite is airborne, it is important to watch it for erratic or unusual flight patterns. If it tends to spin and dive, then the kite is too light for the existing wind conditions. Bring the kite in slowly to avoid possible damage to it.

Another warning signal is a humming line. If the towing line is taut enough to hum and buzz, chances are it is taut enough to break. Bring the kite down carefully, playing it life a fish; when there is slack on the line, pull in gently. Don't force the kite down! This will only cause undue stress on the line. If the line breaks, it could blow your kite away or into the clutches of a kite-eating tree.

WHERE TO FLY A KITE

A flat, open field is an excellent place to fly a kite; with no buildings or uneven landscape to cause unwanted air turbulence, a kiteflier can only experience a pleasant and successful flight. Lake shores and beaches offer the kiteflier exceptional flying conditions. A steady breeze usually comes off the ocean and there are no trees or electrical wires to interrupt a relaxing experience.

Treeless hill tops are ideal, although if you happen to live in the city, finding a hill or any open space may be a problem. Good kiteflying areas in a city are usually at a premium, but empty football stadiums, tennis courts, parks, college campuses, and even roof tops can often offer city dwellers adequate open space.

Never fly a kite in the immediate vicinity of electrical or telephone cables. Keep away from busy roadways and beware of laws prohibiting the flying of kites within a five-mile radius of airports. Don't endanger yourself by kiteflying during a thunderstorm; you might not be as lucky as Ben Franklin.

Should your kite tangle its line in a treetop, give it lots of slack. If you wait patiently, chances are more than likely it will free itself. Continuous pulling and tugging will only result in the eventual loss of your kite. If, after waiting a reasonable length of time, the kite has not untangled itself, leave it. Any venture to rescue the kite by climbing the tree can be risky: the top branches of a tree may be too weak to support your weight.

GETTING IT UP

Most modern kites don't require fliers to run feverishly around in circles to get them off the ground. Actually, the old standard idea of running is one of the most ineffective ways to launch a kite. If done properly, it is possible for you to send your kite soaring from your hand from a stationary position.

Once you have checked your kite for balance and made the appropriate bridle adjustments, you are ready to begin. Stand with the wind at your back and gently toss the kite into the air. When you feel the wind against it, let out some line, being careful not to allow slack, which will result in the loss of control. Begin tugging gently and at the same time quickly releasing small amounts of line to let the kite rise above the ground air turbulence. When it gains an altitude of a hundred feet or more, it is well on its way.

If there is not sufficient wind to launch the kite from your hand, you can still loft it easily with the help of a friend. Hold the kite line while a friend walks down wind about fifty feet. Have your friend hold the kite high over his head.

When a gust of wind hits the kite, it should be quickly released into the air. Pull on the kite line and the kite will soar into a firmer breeze, allowing you to experience the satisfaction of riding the wind on the end of a string.

A challenging but exhilarating experience in kiteflying is when you ride your first "thermal." An air thermal is a current of rising warm air that is trapped on top of a cool air mass, a common occurrence during spring, when cool 'early morning temperatures give way to hot afternoons. When a kite is riding a thermal, it will begin to rise steadily, requiring more and more line as it gains altitude. However, any oncoming breeze can blow the thermal away, leaving a high-flying kite without support. The kiteflier should then be prepared to drop his reel and quickly pull in great lengths of string in an effort to reloft the kite. Unless an unsteady wind arises, the kite should settle down to serious flying at a lower altitude without much delay.

FLYING IN TANDEM

Once you have mastered the techniques of launching a kite, you can expand your kiteflying experience to include the flying of kites in tandem. When you have successfully launched kite number 1 and it is rising steadily, attach the towline on kite number 2 to the towline of kite number 1. The towline for number 2 should be at least six feet in length. Toss the second kite gently into the air, allowing it to catch a breeze. Once it is lofted, slowly release enough of the main towline to give kite number 2 a chance to stabilize. Repeat this process for each kite you wish to add to the train.

There is no limit to the number of kites that can be flown from a single towline. An aerodynamics expert, William R. Bigge, of Washington, D.C., holds the record for the greatest number of kites flown from a single line: in the summer of 1974 Bigge lofted 261 small kites in tandem.

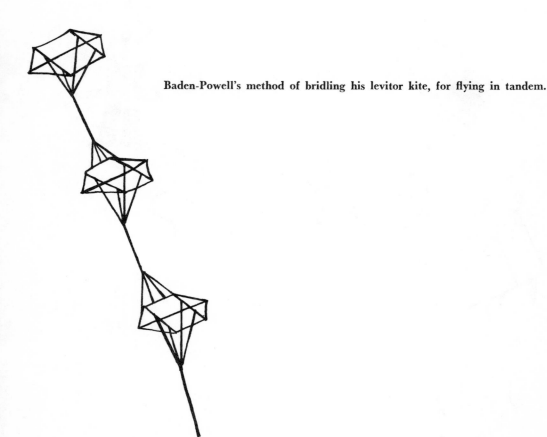

Baden-Powell's method of bridling his levitor kite, for flying in tandem.

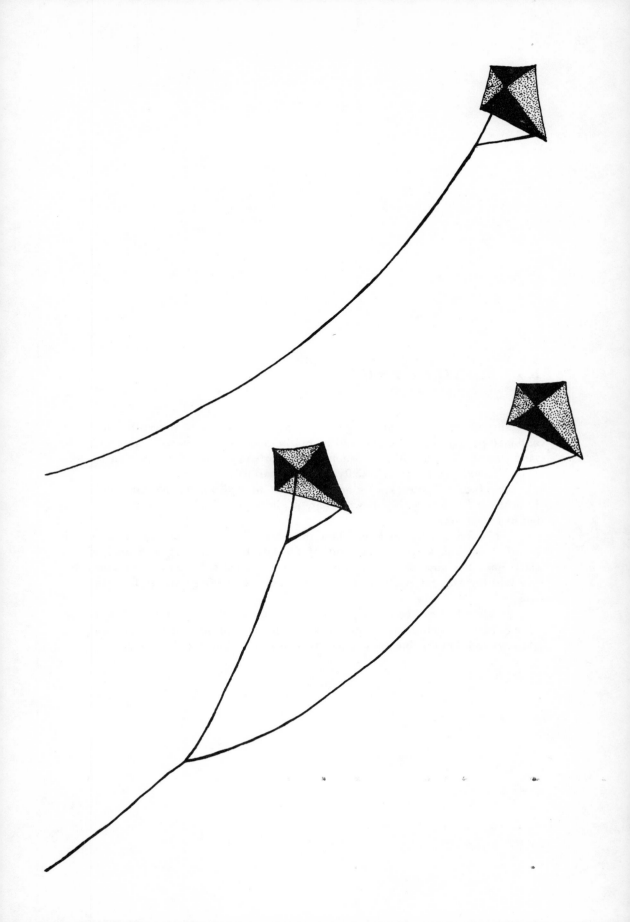

KITE FIGHTING

The ancient art of kite fighting goes back as far as the early sixteenth century. A national pastime in India, the object of the sport is to entangle one's glass- or sand-coated kite line with an opponent's and attempt, through friction on his line, to cut it and leave your own kite flying and unharmed.

The Indian fighter kite is an instrument of delicate balance and precision. Basically a flat kite with a bowed spar, it glides gracefully on the air as it seeks out its challenger.

While flying a fighter kite, follow this basic rule: when the nose of the kite is pointing upward, keep the line taut. If the kite begins to loop and dive, give it slack until the nose is pointing up once again. After some patient practice, you will find the kite extremely maneuverable, easily responding even to fingertip control.

Fighting line can be easily prepared with bits of glass or sand and white glue. Simply run five feet of cotton line through a mixture of one part glue to two parts glass or sand. Let the line dry completely before attaching it to the bridle.

LANDING

Landing a kite safely requires the time and patience. If your kite is flying with stability, it is best to reel in the line as slack occurs. After reeling in small amounts of line, allow the kite some time to restabilize itself before continuing the process. This should prevent any undue stress on the line that could damage the kite.

If the kite's flying pattern becomes erratic, it is best to "walk" it down. Have a friend hold the reel. Then, with a gloved hand holding the line, walk toward the kite. This will shorten the line without reeling it in; eventually, the kite should return directly to your hand.

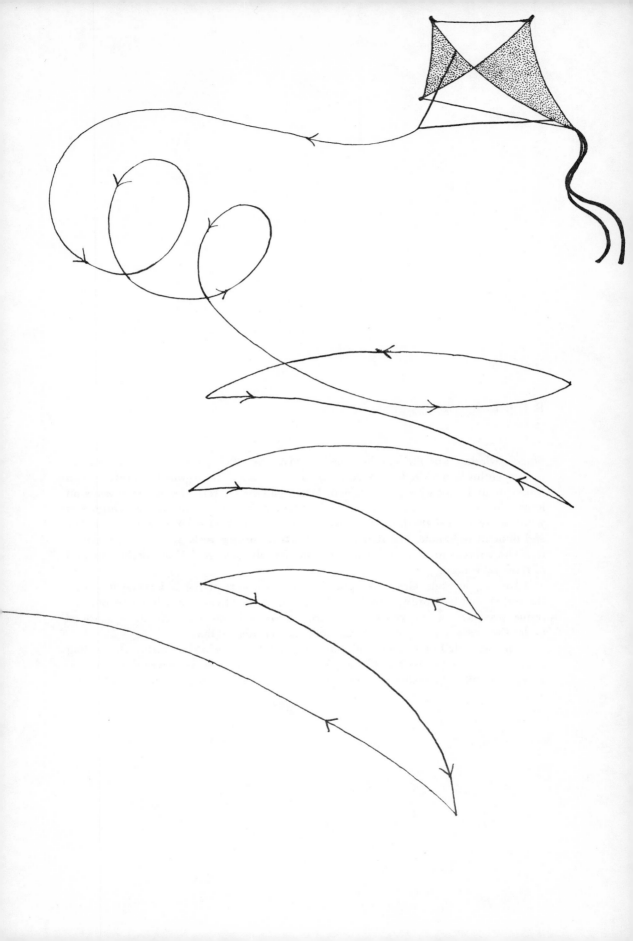

REELS

Since rewinding kite line can be a tedious task, the efficiency of a reel is important to any enthusiastic kiteflier. A reel can be anything from a wooden dowel to an elaborate and expensive power winch. When choosing a reel, the central core is an important factor for you to consider. The larger the core is, the less revolutions it will require to reel the kite in. However, most devices with large cores are heavy and difficult to handle. For that reason, short-rod fishing reels are gaining popularity. The enjoyment of flying a kite is considerably increased if a suitable method of retrieval is used.

Reeling in your kite takes practice. When you're flying a heavy-wind kite, the reel should be sturdily constructed. Reeling in an already taut line can put extreme pressure on the central core and in some instances, reels have snapped under the strain, leaving an unsalvageable mass of tangled line.

Should your kite suddenly display irregular flying behavior during the reeling in process, just play the kite like a fish and reel the line in whenever slack occurs. Have a friend help at the very end by catching the kite to prevent a crash landing.

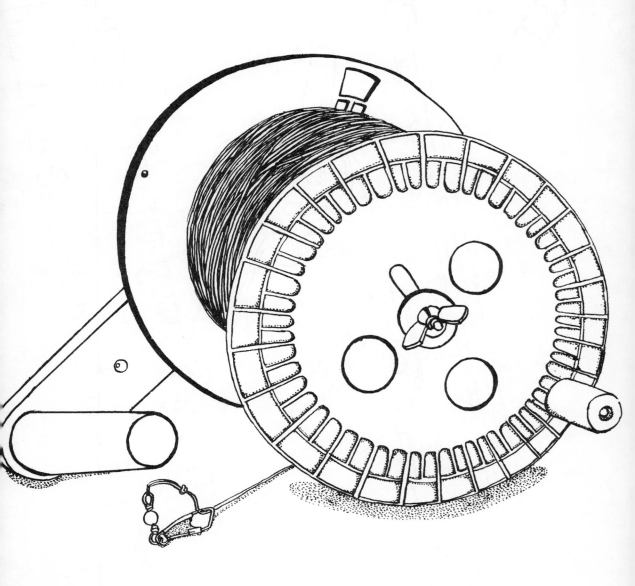

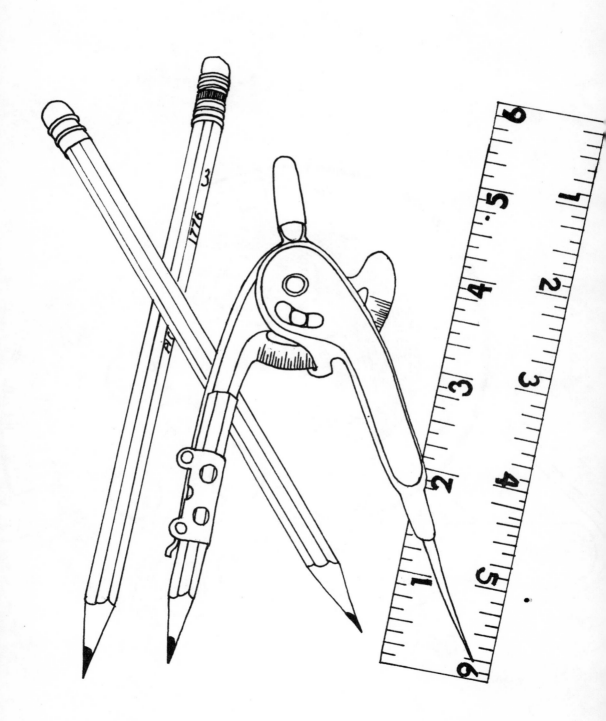

KITE WORKS

Materials and Tools

The first kites made by man that we have evidence of were made of tropical leaves and sticks. Today, kites can be made of paper, plastic such as Mylar, cotton, silk, or sailcloth. They can be as short as or as long as 125 feet. Kites can be designed in any imaginable shape.

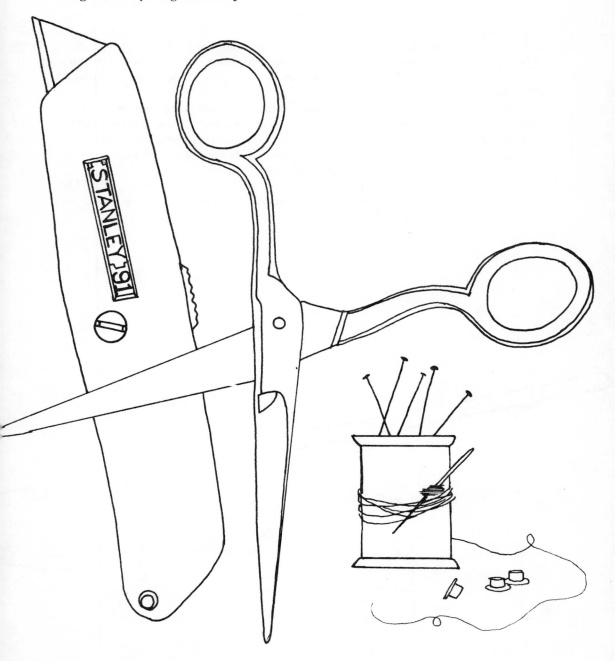

FRAMES

All kites with the exception of the new nonrigid designs, require a frame to give them shape and support. When designing a kite, remember that the lightest and strongest materials should be used for both cover and frame. Soft woods such as white pine or spruce are particularly good for kite spines and spars and are readily available at hobby shops and lumberyards. When the wood strips are round, they are called "dowels."

Most oriental kites have bamboo frames. Bamboo, although difficult to prepare, is perhaps one of the lightest, strongest, and most flexible woods available. Lengths of bamboo can be easily obtained from garden shops or nurseries. A cheap matchstick or slat type bamboo window shade can supply enough wood to make several kite frames; so can slatted table mats.

If purchased in pole form, bamboo must be split and cut into thin strips. The strips can be bent into a wide variety of intricate shapes after being soaked in water or heated over a candle flame.

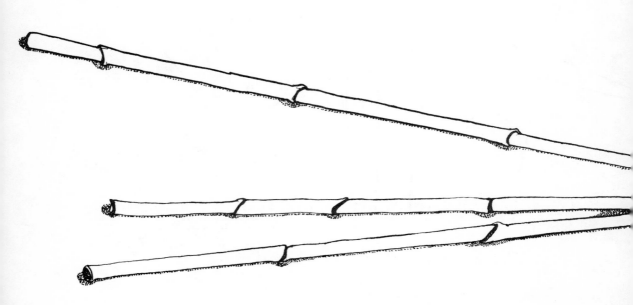

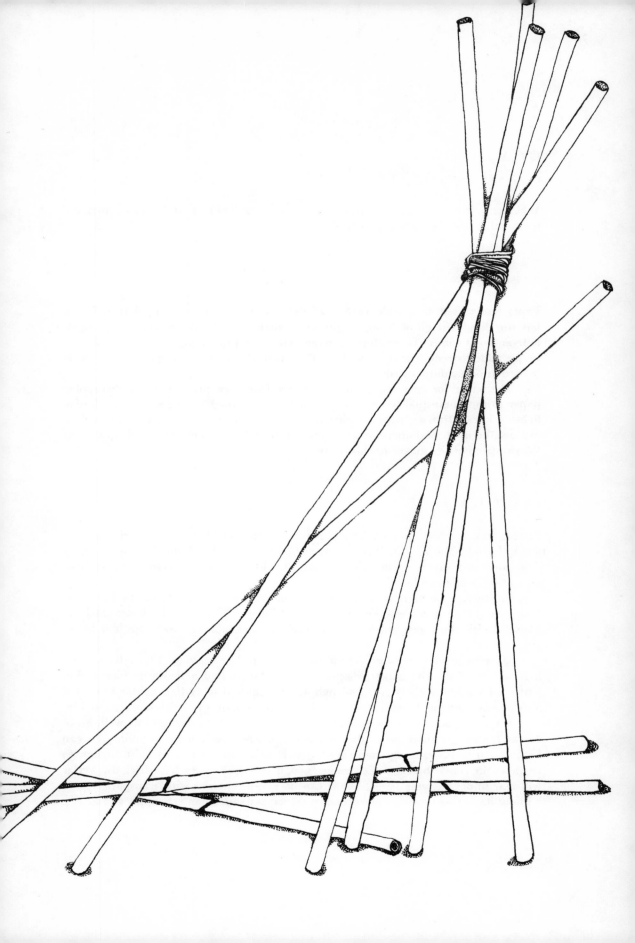

COVERS

Whether you are buying or designing your kite, remember that the cover material is crucial to the kite's flying potential.

PAPER

Paper lends itself to a wide variety of decorations and interesting shapes, but it has the disadvantage of being fragile and should only be flown in three-to-eight-mile-an-hour winds. To reinforce a paper kite, run tape along the edges; this will insure added strength and durability. Tape can also be used to mend any rips or tears that occur during flying.

The paper for covering a kite can range from newsprint or brown wrapping paper to the finest-quality tissue paper such as that used by the makers of Indian fighting kites. Drawing paper, which comes in numerous sizes, weights, and colors, can also be used. Stationery or art-supply stores offer a wide variety of papers for the prospective kite maker to choose from.

PLASTIC

Plastic has become increasingly popular in kite making because of its high strength and light weight. A wide variety of ready-made plastic kites are sold at drugstores and supermarkets. Plastic kites should be flown in winds ranging from six to twelve miles an hour.

Gunther, a German toy manufacturer, offers a line of sturdy plastic kites featuring brightly colored graphics of birds and insects. These can be flown safely in winds of eight to fifteen miles an hour. They are available in kite shops and better toy stores.

Mylar is a relatively new plastic to be used in kite making. Frank Rodriguez, a New York City kite maker, discovered that Mylar had a tensile resilience that lent itself readily to the rigors and maneuvers required of Indian fighter kites and also of long dragon kites. He designed a fifty-five-foot silver Mylar dragon kite that not only glistened in the sunlight, but gleamed in the moonlight as well. Since Mylar is stronger than most other plastics, it is also much more versatile and can be flown in winds ranging from six to twenty miles an hour. It is light enough to be flown in gentle breezes, yet strong enough to stand up to heavy winds. Mylar will tear under extreme stress, but it can be easily repaired with transparent tape without impairing the kite's performance. Mylar is available in art-supply stores.

CLOTH

Cloth lends itself quite readily to kite making. This old stand-by, which gives with the wind's movement, is the strongest kite material available today. Cloth kites can be made of cotton, canvas, sailcloth, Ripstop nylon, or silk. Closely woven cotton is a favorite; it comes in bright colors and patterns and is both easily obtainable and inexpensive. Silk is excellent, but it is hard to work with and very expensive. Ripstop nylon, used for tents and boat sails, is becoming popular for kite making. Strong and light, this fabric is reinforced with heavy-duty thread to prevent rips from enlarging. Check the yellow pages of your phone directory for companies that make sails and camping equipment; they usually have bundles of fabric remnants they want to dispose of.

Decorative Chinese figure kite.

T A P E S

Tapes of various adhesive kinds are useful and versatile commodities in kite making. Scotch Magic tape is light and strong and is what should be used for reinforcing and mending paper or plastic kites. Strapping tape, obtainable at hardware stores, is a strong plastic tape that has been reinforced with fiberglass threads; it is excellent for use on cloth kites, but it is heavy and should be used frugally.

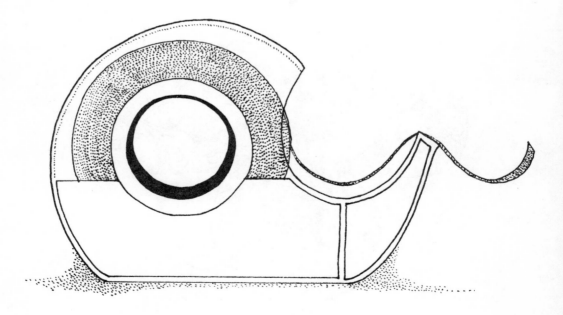

GLUES

When gluing two pieces of wood together for a kite frame, apply a white glue, such as Elmer's Glue-All. To reinforce the joint, wrap a length of string around it and add a second layer of glue. White glue, which is strong and water-resistant, can also be used for gluing a cloth cover to a wooden kite frame. When gluing a paper cover to a kite frame, use rubber cement, tissue paste, or a mixture of flour and water.

WEIGHT

The smaller the kite, the lighter the material used for the frame and cover should be. This is a basic rule of kite making. Heavy material, hardwood, and added ornamentation should be reserved for larger kites.

B A L A N C E

All kites should be symmetrical in area to ensure the best flying results and the horizontal spars must be in perfect balance. You can achieve this by balancing the spar on the blade of a knife and finding its exact center. The vertical spar can be slightly heavier at the bottom; this will help keep the kite stable when in flight by creating drag.

T O O L S

Kite making doesn't require many tools, and those needed are easy to come by: pencils, compass, ruler, tape measure, scissors, utility or craft knife, pliers, grommets, needle and thread, straight pins, small saw, and a clamp.

Construction

The following pages include twenty-three kite designs for you to make. Each of the basic kite groups are represented and many of the kites mentioned in the first section, Kite Tales, will be featured. All you need is some time and the wind at your back to urge you on.

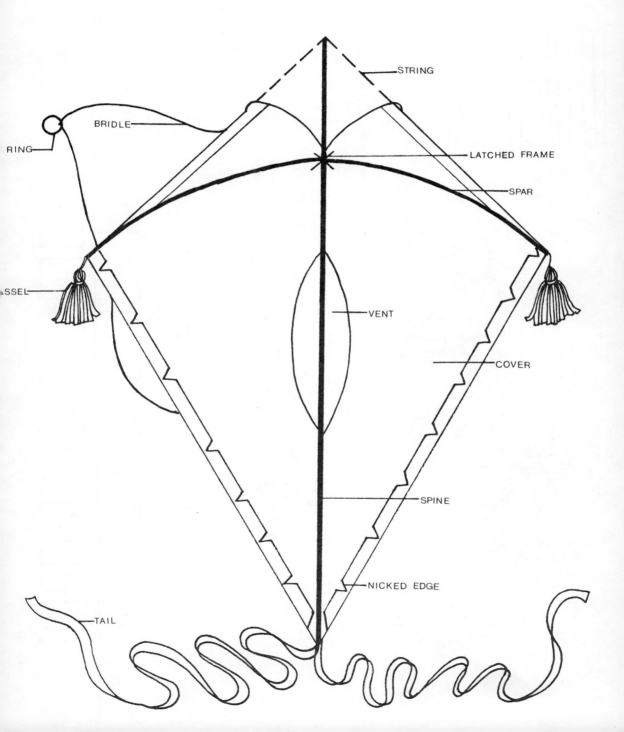

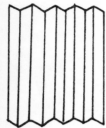

Left to right: 1. Bow tail (paper).
2. Bow tail (cloth).
3. Linen tail.
4. Tassel tail.
5. Ladder tail.
6. Strip tail.

1

2

3

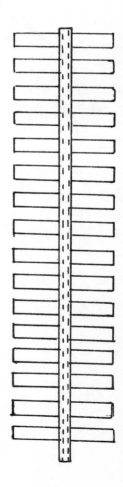

T A I L S

The bow tail (1) is a traditional design that can be made by tying accordion-pleated pieces of paper to a length of string five times the length of the kite.

Another bow tail (2) is essentially the same as the first is but it is made of linen and used mainly for cloth kites. Six-inch-by-one-inch strips of fabric are sewn to a central strip one inch wide and, again, five times the length of the kite.

A strip tail (3) consists simply of long lengths of paper or cloth attached by one end to the base of the kite, with the strips left to fly freely at the other end.

The tassel tail (4) is made up of short strips of cloth or paper that are tied to a length of kite line and then attached to the base of the kite. This tail is recommended for parafoils.

The remaining two tails (which can be made in cloth or paper) are ideal for square or rectangular kites; the ladder tail (5) and the ribbon tail (6) are both popular Japanese designs.

4

5

6

KNOTS

Sailors' knots are used frequently in the construction of kites. Whether they are used to attach the towline to the bridle or simply used to make bows for the tail, the following knots are essential for every kiteflier to be familiar with:

    1. Overhand knot—a multipurpose knot.

    2. Thief's knot—a multipurpose knot.

    3. Clove hitch—a knot used in tail making.

    4. Running bowline knot—a knot used for tying the towline to the bridle.

    5a,b. Lark's head knot—a knot used for attaching the bridle to a tow ring, which in turn is attached to the towline. (The tow ring is a small plastic ring easily obtainable wherever curtain rods are sold.)

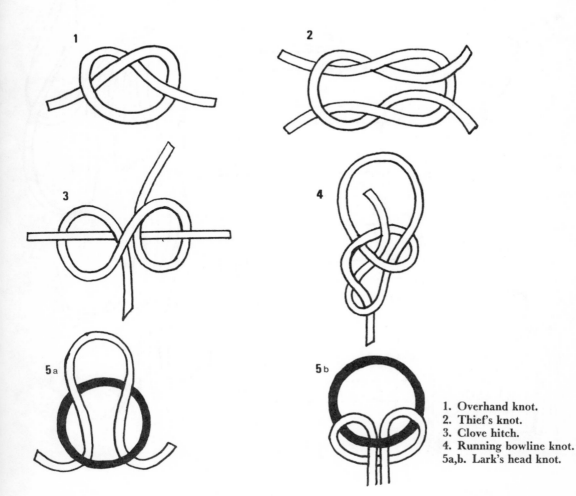

1. Overhand knot.
2. Thief's knot.
3. Clove hitch.
4. Running bowline knot.
5a,b. Lark's head knot.

NOTCHING AND BRACING

When a kite design requires a brace line, the following types of notches will be required. (You can use a regular paring knife, utility knife, or small saw to make the notches.)

1. Slot notch—used for soft- and hardwoods.
2. V-notch—often used for bamboo.
3. Square notch—used for attaching two pieces of wood together.

If the design calls for the spars to be joined to the spine, a method of cross bracing is required. This is done by winding a length of string around the joint (4) and covering the connection with a thick layer of white glue; this will secure the joint firmly.

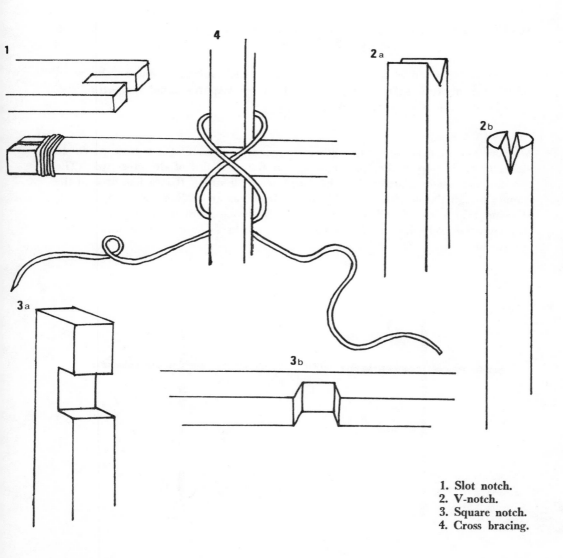

1. Slot notch.
2. V-notch.
3. Square notch.
4. Cross bracing.

DIAMOND KITE

FRAME: 2 softwood dowels.
              spine, 32 by ⅛ in.
              spar, 28 by ⅛ in.

COVER: cloth, newsprint, or tissue paper (1 sheet) 3 ft. sq.

LINE: for cloth, 20 lb. test.
           for paper, 10 lb. test.

BRIDLE: 2 legs.

TAIL: bow tail.

WIND: for cloth, 8–24 mph.
          for paper, 3–10 mph.

MATERIALS: scissors, pencil, ruler, needle and thread, white glue, tow ring,
                  saw or utility knife.

The classic diamond shape comes to most people's minds whenever the word "kite" is mentioned. Like all flat kites, this design requires a tail for extra drag. The diamond kite is a low-angle flier.

CONSTRUCTION

Measure and cut the spine and spar; V-notch the ends. Cut a square notch 10 inches from the top of the spine and also at the midpoint of the cross spar. The two dowels must be glued and latched together with string. Run a line around the frame through the notched ends. Using the frame as an outline cut out the cover, allowing 1 inch all around for a hem. Attach the cover to the frame by turning the hem around the frame and gluing it. Add the bridle, using needle and thread, and the tow ring.

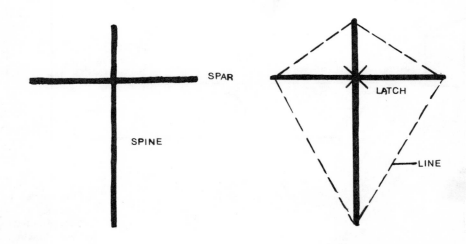

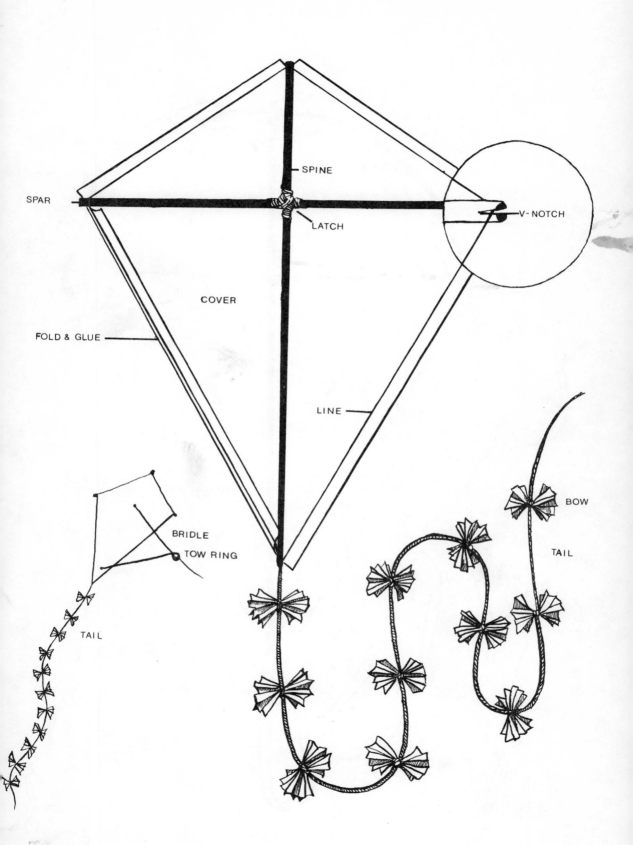

SPINE

SPAR

LATCH

V-NOTCH

COVER

FOLD & GLUE

LINE

BRIDLE

TOW RING

BOW

TAIL

TAIL

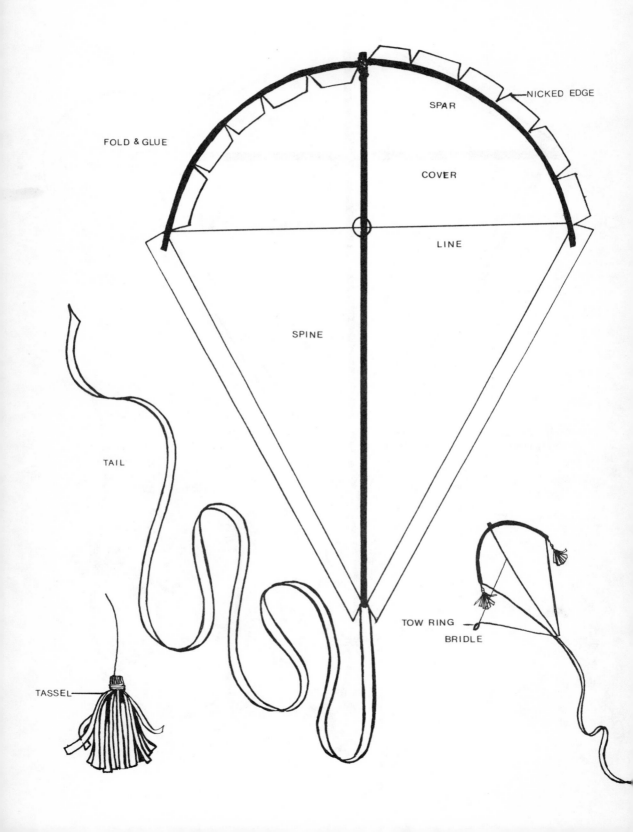

NICKED EDGE

SPAR

FOLD & GLUE

COVER

LINE

SPINE

TAIL

TOW RING

BRIDLE

TASSEL

ARCH-TOP KITE

FRAME: 2 bamboo strips or softwood dowels.
                spine, 32 by $\frac{1}{8}$ in.
                arch top, 32 by $\frac{1}{8}$ in.

COVER: cloth or paper (1 sheet) 36 in. sq.

LINE: for cloth, 20 lb. test.
           for paper, 10 lb. test.

BRIDLE: 2 legs.

TAIL: ribbon tail.

WIND: for cloth, 8–24 mph.
            for paper, 3–7 mph.

MATERIALS: scissors, pencil, ruler, needle and thread, candle, white glue, tow
                    ring, 2 tassels, saw or utility knife.

The arch-top kite is one of the oldest European designs, dating back to the 1600s. It was used by George Pocock in the early 1800s for his experiments with kite towing. Pocock even designed a collapsible version for his charvolant.

CONSTRUCTION

Notch ends of the sticks. To prepare the arch top, carefully heat the wood over a candle flame or soak it in hot water, then bend it. Tie the ends of the arch with string. Cut a square notch 1 inch below the top of the spine and latch it, with string and glue, to the midpoint of the arch. Run a line around the frame, as done in the diamond kite. Use the frame as an outline for cutting out the cover, allowing 1 inch all around for the hem. Attach cover to frame with glue. Add the bridle, using needle and thread, and tow ring. Attach a long ribbon for the tail. The addition of the side tassels is optional.

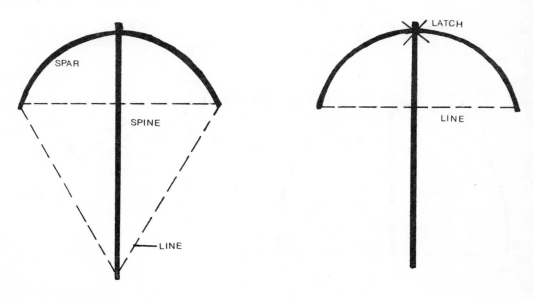

DRAGON KITE

FRAME: 1 bamboo or rattan strip, 34 by ⅛ by ⅛ in.
1 softwood dowel, 14 by ⅛ in.

COVER: paper, Mylar, or crepe paper, 15 in. by 25 ft.

LINE: for paper, 10 lb. test.
for Mylar, 20 lb. test.

BRIDLE: two legs.

TAIL: none.

WIND: 5–20 mph.

MATERIALS: scissors, pencil, ruler, needle and thread, strapping tape, white glue, tow ring, saw or utility knife.

The dragon kite dances in the air as it flies. One of the easiest kites to fly, this design has tremendous stability thanks to its long, flowing tail.

CONSTRUCTION

Arch the bamboo or rattan strip and secure with string (see p. 93). Cut a square notch near one end of the dowel and latch it with string and glue to the mid-point on the arch strip. Use the frame as an outline to cut out the top of the cover, nicking it to fit the curve; allow an extra inch for turning. Cut and glue this to the frame. Cut and taper the remaining length of cover material (approximately 23½ feet) to a point and allow it to flow freely. Run a strip of strapping tape down the tail on both its back and front; this will prevent twisting during flight. Add the bridle, using needle and thread, and the tow ring and streamers if you like.

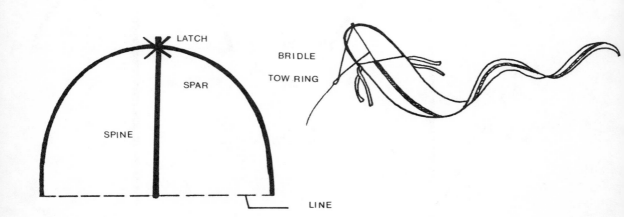

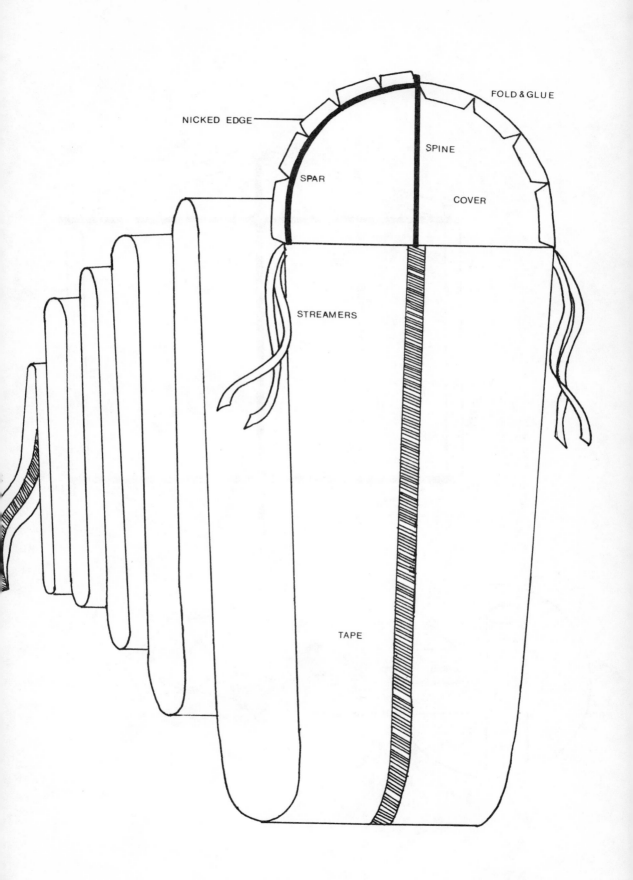

NICKED EDGE

FOLD & GLUE

SPINE

SPAR

COVER

STREAMERS

TAPE

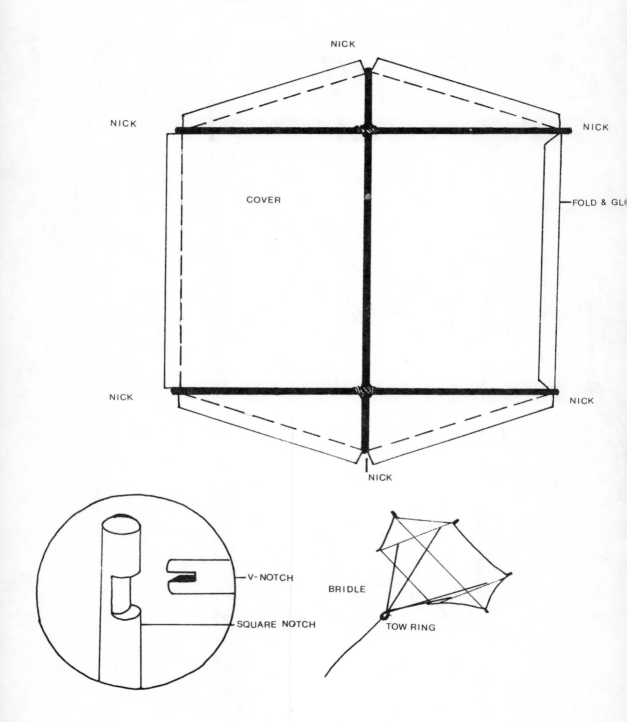

NICK

NICK

NICK

COVER

FOLD & GL

NICK

NICK

NICK

V-NOTCH

SQUARE NOTCH

BRIDLE

TOW RING

LEVITOR KITE

FRAME: 3 softwood dowels, 36 by ¼ in.

COVER: cloth, 42 by 45 in.

LINE: 30 lb. test.

BRIDLE: 4 legs.

TAIL: none.

WIND: 15–25 mph.

MATERIALS: scissors, pencil, ruler, needle and thread, white glue, 2 tow rings, saw or utility knife.

The levitor kite was designed by B. F. S. Baden-Powell in the early 1890s. Flown in a six-unit train, the kite was used to lift men into the air for observation during the Boer War.

CONSTRUCTION

The ends of all the spars should be V-notched. Cut square notches in the centers of the two horizontal spars and square notches 6 inches in from either end of the vertical spar (the spine). Latch the horizontal spars to the spine with glue and string. Run a line around the frame through the V-notches. Cut the cover, allowing an extra inch all around. Turn down the hem of the cover and glue it to the frame. Attach the bridle, using needle and thread, and add tow rings, using four lark's head knots.

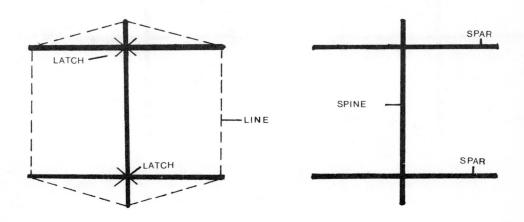

BEN FRANKLIN'S KITE

FRAME: 2 light cedar strips,
              (long enough to reach the ends of a man's silk handkerchief)

COVER: 1 man's silk handkerchief.

LINE: 20 lb. test.

BRIDLE: 2 legs.

TAIL: none.

WIND: 5–20 mph.

MATERIALS: none.

CONSTRUCTION

Cross and latch the center of the two cedar strips. Tie the corners of the handkerchief to the extremities of the cross. When a bridle, tow ring, tail, and line are attached, it will rise steadily in the air, like those made of paper. But being made of silk, it is better able to stand up to wet winds of a rain storm without tearing.*

(Remember, never fly this or any other kite during a thunderstorm; it will attract lightning and cause serious personal injury.)

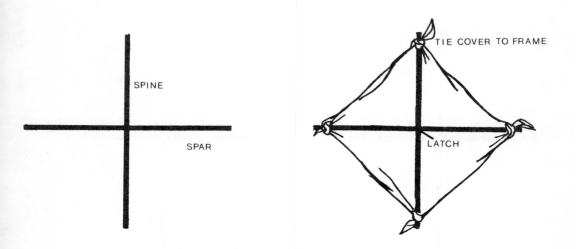

SPINE

SPAR

TIE COVER TO FRAME

LATCH

* Adapted from Benjamin Franklin, **PAPERS, vol. IV, pp. 360–69.**

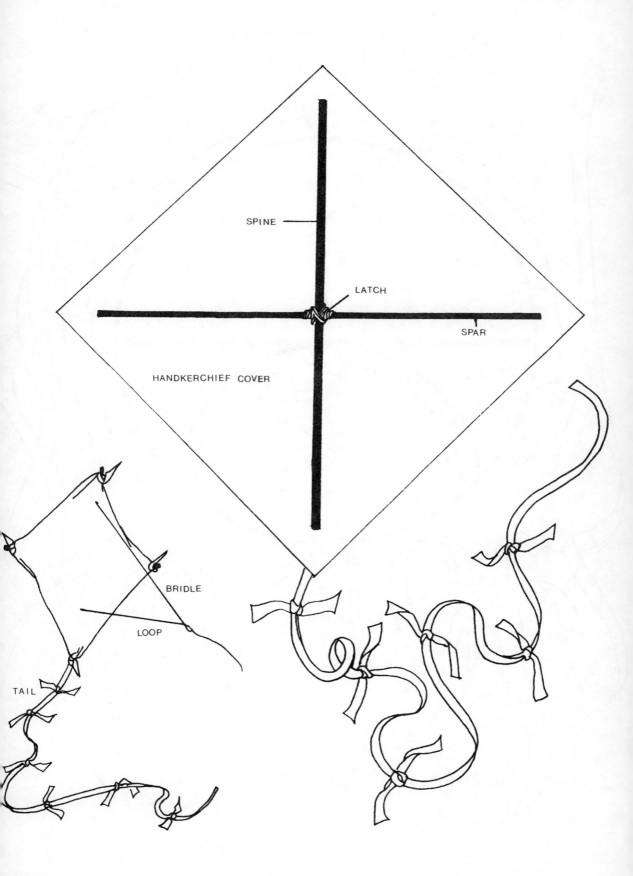

SPINE

LATCH

SPAR

HANDKERCHIEF COVER

BRIDLE

LOOP

TAIL

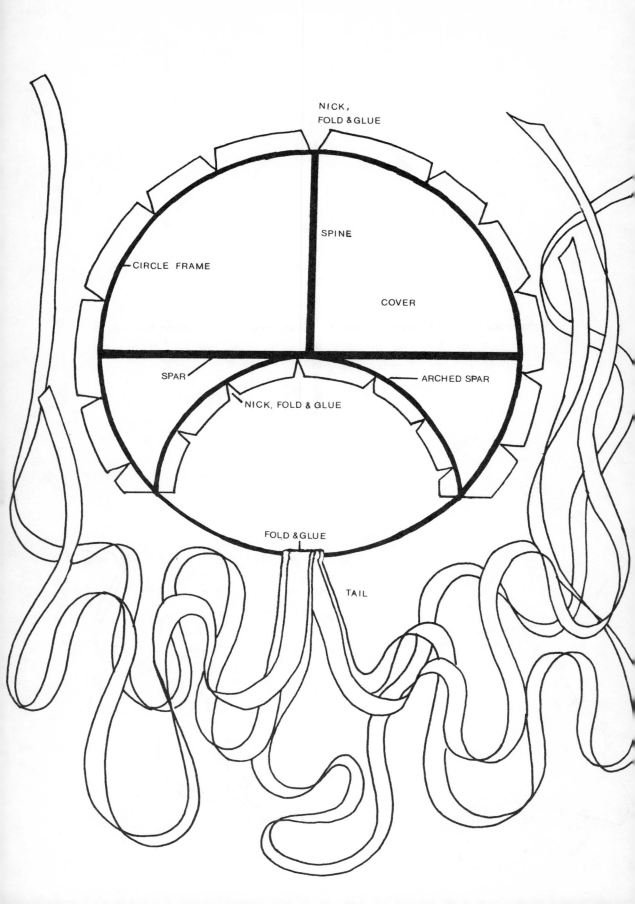

HAWAIIAN CIRCLE KITE

FRAME: 4 bamboo or rattan strips.
round edge, 4 ft. 9 in. by ⅛ in.
small crescent, 1 ft. 4 in. by ⅛ in.
vertical spar, 10 by ⅛ in.
horizontal spar, 1 ft. 8 in. by ⅛ in.

COVER: tissue or tracing paper, 1½ ft. sq.

LINE: 20 lb. test.

BRIDLE: 3 legs.

TAIL: 5 strips of crepe paper, 10 ft. by 1 in.

WIND: 5–12 mph.

MATERIALS: scissors, pencil, ruler, needle and thread, white glue, tow ring, saw or utility knife.

This kite is easy to fly and interesting to watch as it gracefully dips and glides over the countryside. It is a light-wind kite.

CONSTRUCTION

Tie and glue the ends of the outer circle spar together (see p. 76). Notch and secure in place, with string and glue, the small crescent and the vertical and horizontal spars. When the frame is dry, outline the kite frame on a large piece of tissue or tracing paper. Cut out the cover, allowing an extra inch all around for hemming. Cut a series of nicks around the cover to insure smooth attachment to the outer circle and the crescent. Position the frame on the paper, fold over the frame, and glue the nicked flaps down. Attach the bridle, using needle and thread, tow ring, and tail.

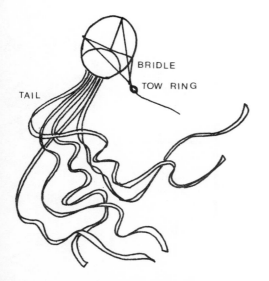

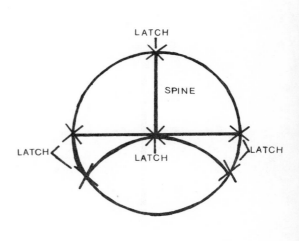

MALAY KITE

FRAME: 2 bamboo strips, 24 by ⅛ by ⅛ in.

COVER: light paper, 25 in. sq.

LINE: 15 lb. test.

BRIDLE: 3 legs.

TAIL: none.

WIND: 3–7 mph.

MATERIALS: scissors, pencil, ruler, needle and thread, white glue, tow ring, saw or utility knife.

The Malay kite is the earliest form of a bowed kite. It is a light-wind kite and amazingly maneuverable. The basis for the famed Eddy kite, it is a close cousin to the Indian fighter kite.

CONSTRUCTION

Latch the mid-points of the strips together with string and glue to form a cross. The ends of the strips must be notched, so as to accommodate a string frame. Place the frame on the paper. Allowing an extra inch all around, cut out the cover, fold over the edges, and glue it to the frame. Bow horizontal spar as shown in the diagram, and secure with a piece of string. Attach the bridle, using needle and thread, and tow ring.

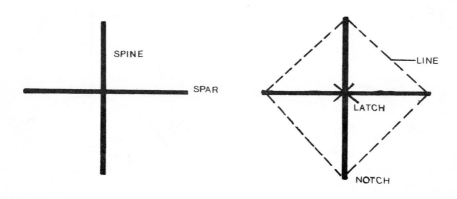

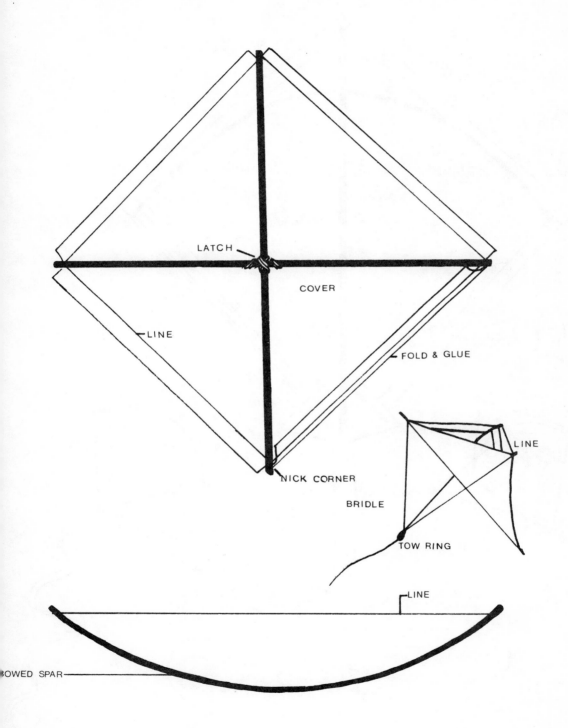

LATCH

COVER

LINE

FOLD & GLUE

NICK CORNER

BRIDLE

LINE

TOW RING

LINE

BOWED SPAR

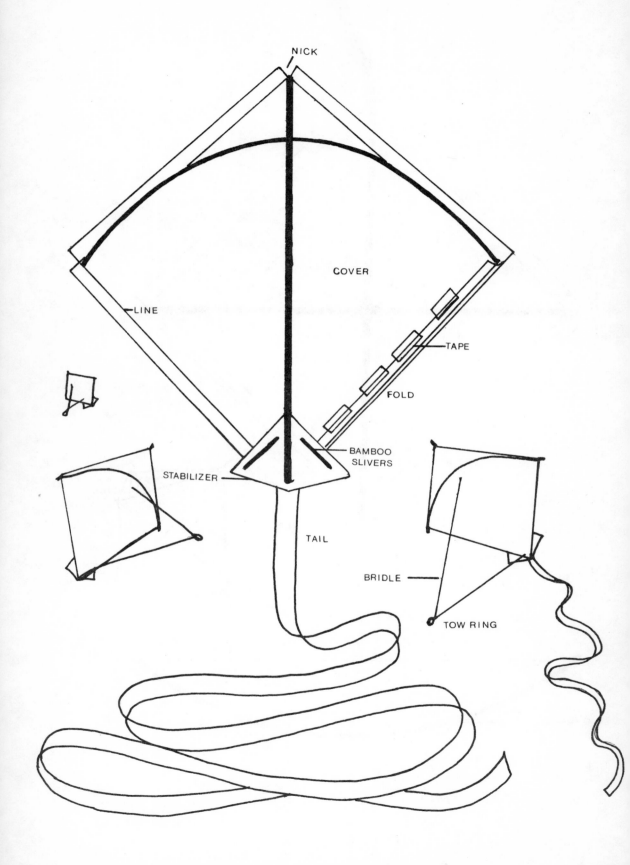

INDIAN FIGHTER

FRAME: 2 bamboo strips.
  spine, 23 by ¼ by ⅛ in.
  spar, 33 by ¼ by ⅛ in.

COVER: tissue paper or Mylar (one sheet), 34 by 23 in. (Use scraps for stabilizer.)

LINE: 10 lb. test.

BRIDLE: none.

TAIL: tissue paper, 10 ft. by 1 in. strips (optional).

WIND: 5–15 mph.

MATERIALS: scissors, pencil, ruler, needle and thread, 2 4-in. slivers of bamboo, tape, white glue, sandpaper, saw or utility knife.

The Indian fighter kite is one of the most challenging kites to fly, but once you have mastered the technique, it will always be a favorite. When you are learning to maneuver this kite, it might be to your advantage to add a tail; this will help slow the kite's movement down and enable you to get the hang of it.

CONSTRUCTION

Split and cut the bamboo strips to size. Band the spar into a bow and latch its mid-point to a point 4 inches from the top of the spine. Using the frame as your guide, lay out and cut cover material, leaving an extra inch all around. Attach cover to frame with tape. Cut out a stabilizer 5 inches long by 7½ inches wide. Glue the slivers of bamboo to the stabilizer and the stabilizer to the base of the kite. Attach the bridle with needle and thread. Reinforce bridle points with tape.

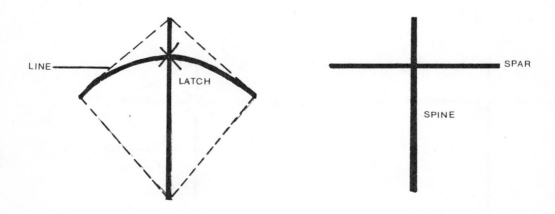

E D D Y   K I T E

FRAME: 2 softwood or hardwood dowels.
               spine, 36 by ¼ in.
               spar, 36 by ½ in.

COVER: light cloth or paper, 38 in. sq.

LINE: for cloth, 20 lb. test.
        for paper, 10 lb. test.

BRIDLE: 2 legs.

TAIL: none.

WIND: for cloth, 8–25 mph.
        for paper, 5–15 mph.

MATERIALS: scissors, pencil, ruler, needle and thread, white glue, tow ring, saw
                 or utility knife.

When a flat kite is changed into a bowed kite, a new aerodynamic factor called "dihedral angle" is introduced. A dihedral angle is the angle formed at the meeting of two supporting planes. Like birds, when a kite has a dihedral angle, it is more stable and a better flier. This famous bowed kite was designed by William Eddy in the 1890s.

CONSTRUCTION

Notch the ends of the dowels. Bow the spar as shown in the diagram. Secure the mid-point of the bowed spar to a point 7 inches from the top of the spine with string. Run a line around the frame. Use the frame as a guide for cutting out the cover. Allow for an extra inch all around for hemming. Glue the cover to the frame. Attach the bridle (with needle and thread) through the cover to the frame. Add tow ring.

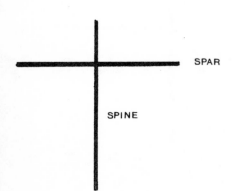

SPAR

SPINE

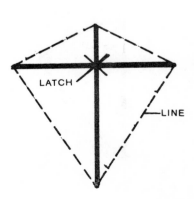

LATCH

LINE

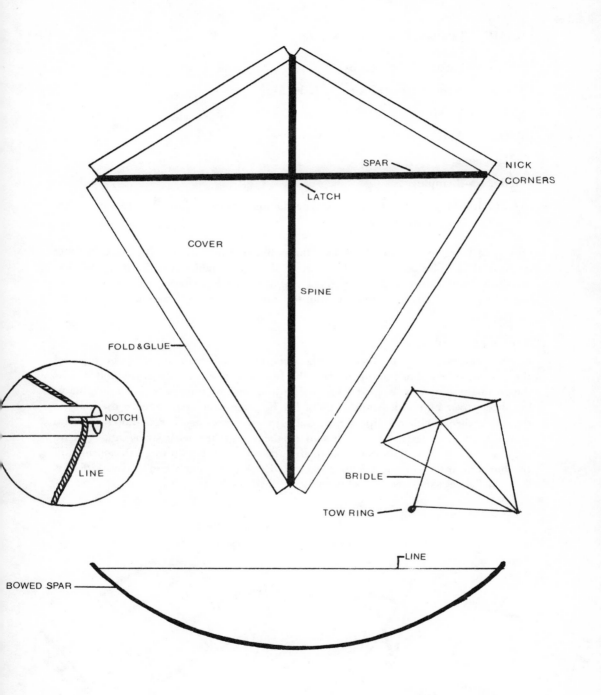

SPAR

NICK
CORNERS

LATCH

COVER

SPINE

FOLD&GLUE

NOTCH

LINE

BRIDLE

TOW RING

LINE

BOWED SPAR

BOX KITE

FRAME: 8 softwood or hardwood strips.
4 spars, 36 by ¼ by ¼ in.
4 spars, 17 by ¼ by ¼ in.

COVER: cloth or paper (2 sheets), 13 by 51 in.

LINE: 30 lb. test.

BRIDLE: 2 or 4 legs.

TAIL: none.

WIND: 5–25 mph.

MATERIALS: scissors, pencil, ruler, needle and thread, white glue, saw or utility knife, tow ring.

Lawrence Hargrave invented the first three-dimensional kite, the box kite, in 1892 in Australia. [The box kite, being one of the most stable kites built up to that time, was used (after Eddy's) by the U. S. Weather Bureau for testing. This kite has lifted heavy test instruments into the air allowing exploration at high altitudes.]

CONSTRUCTION

Lay out one sheet of the cover material, glue over ½-inch hem along the top and the bottom edge. Glue the top part of the four long spars to the cover material as shown in the diagram. Repeat with the bottom part of the spars and the remaining sheet cover material. Allow 12½ inches between each spar. Secure the ends of the cover sheets with a strip of tape and glue the box together. V-notch the end of the four short spars and latch two of them together with string and glue to form a cross. Repeat this process with the other two spars. To force the corners of the box kite into position, wedge the crossed spars into each end of the kite. Attach the bridle, using needle and thread, and tow ring.

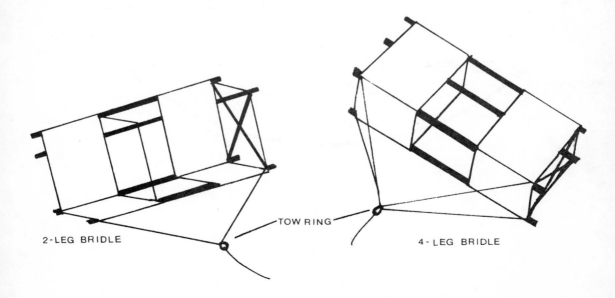

2-LEG BRIDLE   TOW RING   4-LEG BRIDLE

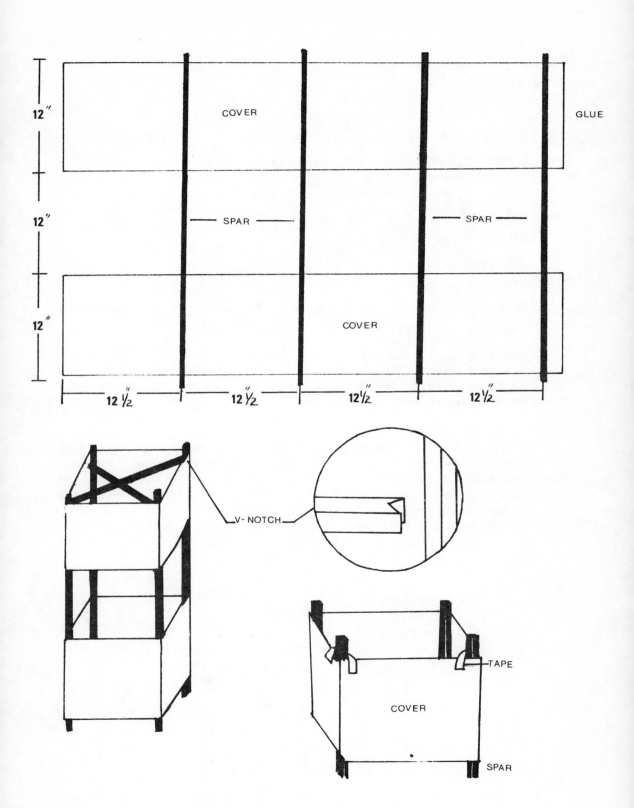

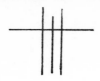

CONYNE KITE

FRAME: 4 softwood or hardwood dowels, 36 by ¼ in.

COVER: lightweight cotton or Ripstop nylon.
1 piece, 40 by 40 in.
2 pieces, 23 by 14 in.

LINE: 20 lb. test.

BRIDLE: 2 legs.

TAIL: none.

WIND: 7–25 mph.

MATERIALS: scissors, pencil, ruler, cotton for pockets (¼ yd.), needle and thread, tow ring, saw or utility knife.

The Conyne kite was invented by Silas J. Conyne in the early 1900s. Basically, it is a winged triangular box kite and a stable flier suited for medium winds. The French Army used the kite for aerial photography so it is better known as the French military box kite.

CONSTRUCTION

Cut spars to size. Following the diagram, cut out cover material, allowing 1 inch all around for hemming. Cut out center square, nick corners, turn in, and hem. Using the pattern, cut and stitch pockets to points indicated on the diagram. Cut out two keel sections (see p. 111), hem top and bottom of each. Fold in half and sew a 1-inch seam down the center of each keel; this will hold the spar in place. Stitch the pockets to main cover to hold the cross spar. Sew the two keels to the main cover. Insert the spars. Stitch pockets closed. Insert cross back spar. Attach the bridle, using needle and thread, and tow ring.

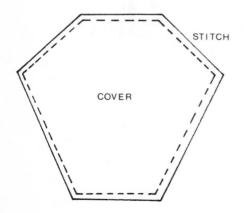

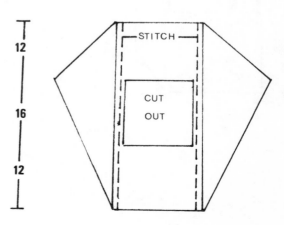

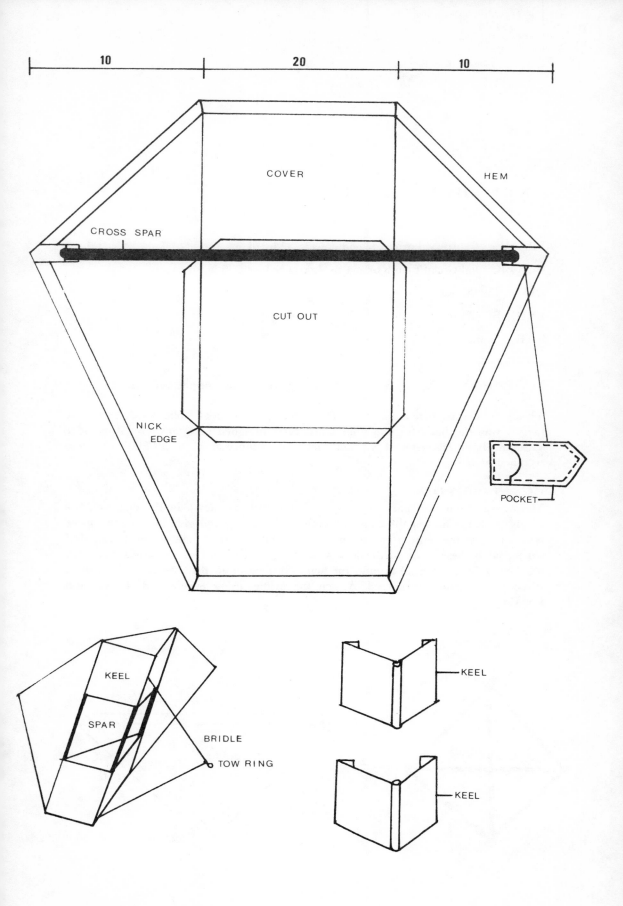

TETRAHEDRAL KITE

FRAME: 6 softwood or hardwood dowels, 32 by ¼ in.

COVER: lightweight cloth or plastic (garbage bag), 36 in. sq.

LINE: 20 lb. test.

BRIDLE: 2 legs.

TAIL: none.

WIND: 7–18 mph.

MATERIALS: white glue, tow ring, saw or utility knife, needle and thread.

This kite, shaped like a regular tetrahedron (a four-sided solid with triangular faces), was the basis for the multicelled kites designed and flown by Alexander Graham Bell. His framed Cygnet kite was comprised of over 4,000 of these tetrahedral cells.

CONSTRUCTION

Measure and cut the spars to size. Notch the ends as shown in the diagram. Securely latch the tops of three spars together with string and glue. Spread the three spars apart at the bottom and fit in the other three spars to obtain the tetrahedral shape; latch these spars to the legs with string and glue. Cut out cover material, allowing 1 inch extra all around for hem. Glue cover to three sides of the frame, leaving the bottom uncovered. Attach the bridle, using needle and thread, and tow ring.

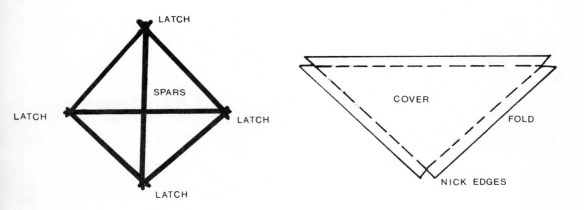

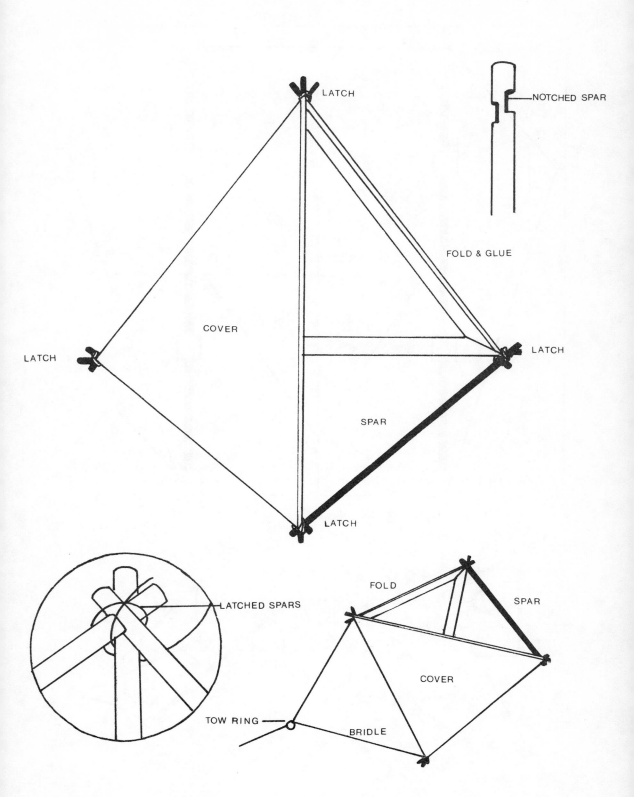

LATCH

NOTCHED SPAR

FOLD & GLUE

COVER

LATCH

LATCH

SPAR

LATCH

LATCHED SPARS

FOLD

SPAR

COVER

TOW RING

BRIDLE

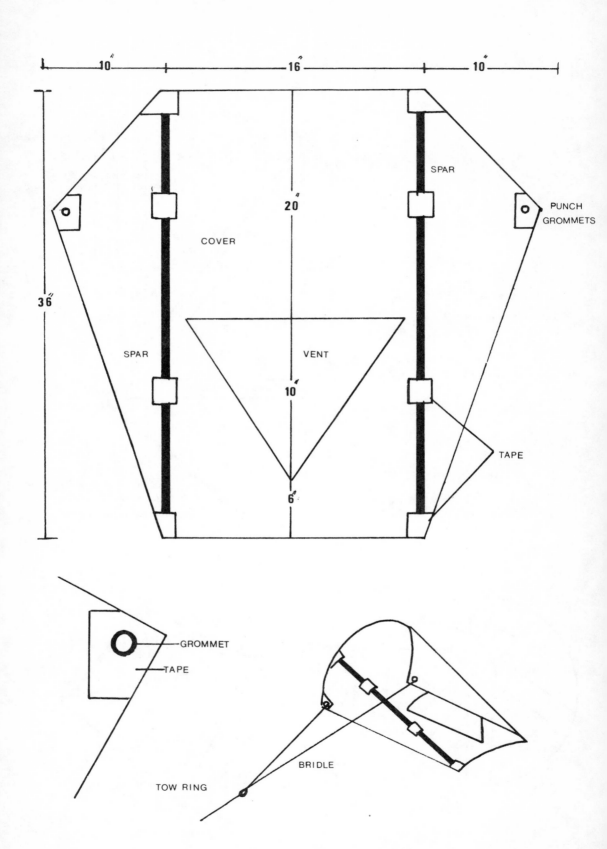

SCOTT SLED

FRAME: 2 softwood or hardwood dowels, 36 by ¼ in.

COVER: plastic (garbage bag or Mylar) sheet, 36 in. sq.

LINE: 20 lb. test.

BRIDLE: 2 legs.

TAIL: none.

WIND: 5–18 mph.

MATERIALS: scissors, pencil, ruler, needle and thread, strapping tape, grommets (see p. 114), tow ring, saw or utility knife.

The Scott sled, first designed by W. M. Allison in 1950 and one of the first soft kites, was brought to the public's attention by Frank Scott, for whom it was named. The sled is an all-wind kite that delicately balances on the edge of the wind.

CONSTRUCTION

Cut spars to size. Following the dimensions shown in the diagram, cut out cover material. Cut out V-shaped vent and tape spars to the cover as shown. Reinforce bridle points with tape and punch in grommets. Attach the bridle, using needle and thread, and tow ring.

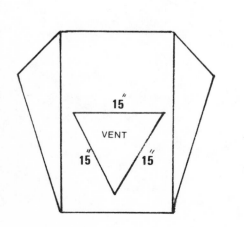

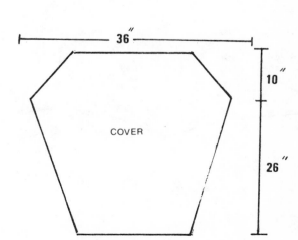

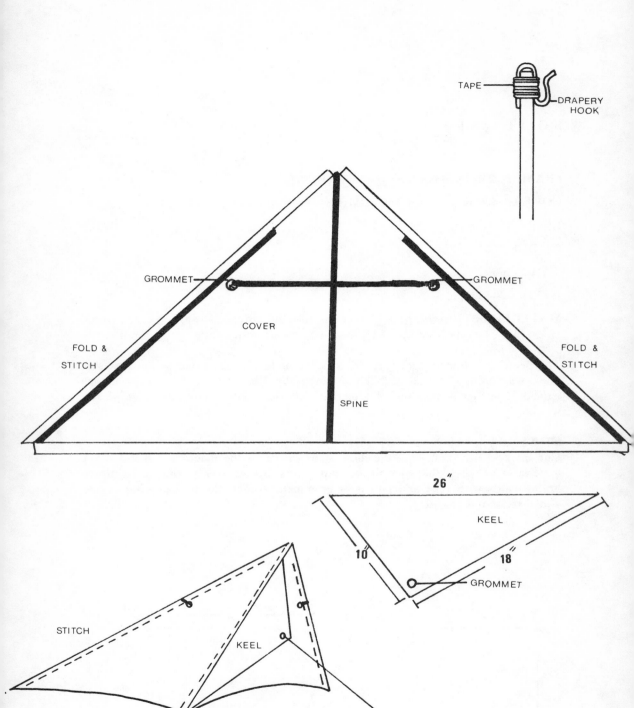

TAPE

DRAPERY HOOK

GROMMET

GROMMET

COVER

FOLD & STITCH

FOLD & STITCH

SPINE

26″

KEEL

10″

18″

GROMMET

STITCH

KEEL

DELTA-WING KITE

FRAME: 4 hardwood dowels.
           2 side spars, 36 by ¼ in.
           1 spine, 28 by ¼ in.
           1 cross spar, 25 by ¼ in.

COVER: plastic or cloth, 36 by 72 in. (keel, 20 in. sq.).

LINE: 50 lb. test.

BRIDLE: 1 leg (attached to keel).

WIND: 10–30 mph.

MATERIALS: scissors, pencil, ruler, needle and thread, grommets, drapery hooks, saw or utility knife.

The delta-wing kite flies flat on the wind as opposed to against it. One of the most stable new designs, this kite, as well as the parawing, was the forerunner of the hang glider. Delta-wing kites are easy to fly and graceful while airborne.

CONSTRUCTION

Cut and measure spine and spars to size. Allowing an inch for hemming, cut out cover material to the dimensions indicated. The keel should also be cut out at this time. Fold the cover triangle shape in half, sandwich the longest section of the keel between the cover fold. Stitch in ¼ inch from the edge through three thicknesses of fabric down the length of the folded center area. Now the keel is attached to the cover surface and a pocket has been made to hold the dowel for the spine. Fold over the sides of the triangle to make pockets for the side spars, insert all three spars and stitch the ends closed. Attach drapery hooks to each end of the cross spar securing with tape. Punch grommets into cover fabric and keel as indicated in the drawing. Insert cross spar to cover opening provided by grommets. Attach the line directly to the keel.

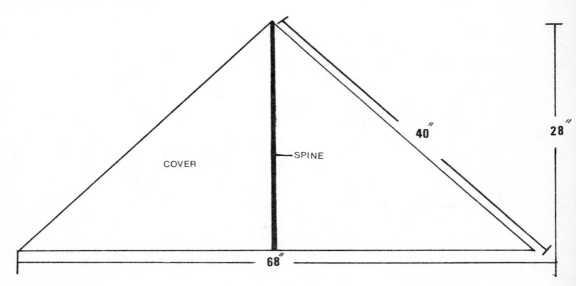

PARAWING

FRAME: none.

COVER: plastic sheeting, 3-mil Mylar, 15 in. sq.

LINE: 20 lb. test.

BRIDLE: 6 legs.

TAIL: Mylar strip, 36 in.

WIND: 5–15 mph.

MATERIALS: scissors, pencil, ruler, needle and thread, tape.

This kite was designed by Francis Rogallo to conform to the wind. Without any frame, this new "soft kite" gets its shape primarily from the fold down the center and the positioning of the bridle.

CONSTRUCTION
Cut cover material to size. Fold the cover diagonally, making a strong crease. Attach bridle lines as indicated, with needle and thread. Make sure the length of the bridle lines are precise (see diagram) and attached to the indicated points. You might want to reinforce the points of attachment with tape. Attach a length of string for tail.

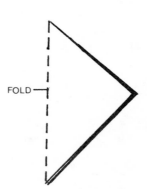

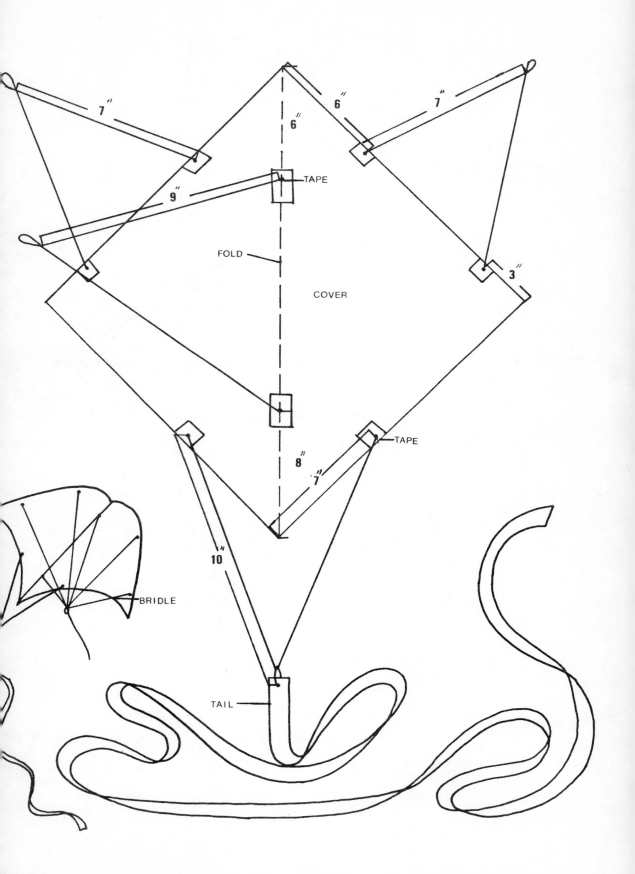

7″

6″

6″

7″

TAPE

9″

FOLD

COVER

3″

TAPE

8″

7″

BRIDLE

10″

TAIL

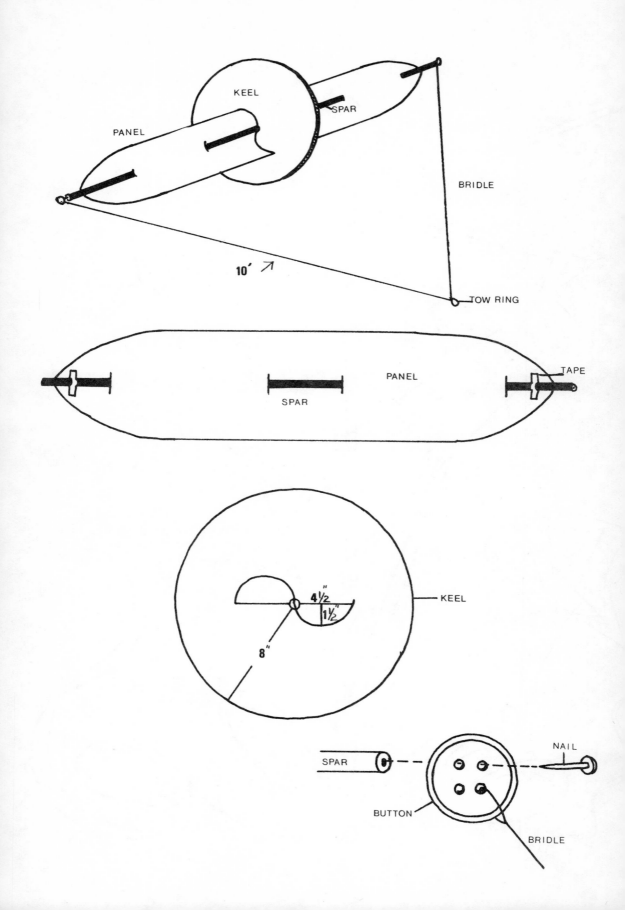

KEEL

SPAR

PANEL

BRIDLE

10'

TOW RING

PANEL

TAPE

SPAR

KEEL

4½"

1½"

8"

SPAR

NAIL

BUTTON

BRIDLE

ROTO KITE

FRAME: 1 hardwood dowel, 28 by ¼ in.

COVER: 2 pieces of 3-ply cardboard.
oval, 10 by 28 in.
circle, 15 in. diam.

LINE: 30 lb. test.

BRIDLE: 2 legs.

TAIL: none.

WIND: 10–25 mph.

MATERIALS: scissors, pencil, ruler, needle and thread, 2 4-hole buttons, white glue, tape, 2 large-head nails, saw or utility knife.

This particular pattern for a roto kite was designed by a friend and fellow kite enthusiast, Theodore T. Kuklinski, who used it as part of a special kite course he taught at the MIT Kite Experimentation Laboratory. Kuklinski flew his Bicentennial edition of the roto kite at the 1976 Boston Kite Festival and received special recognition.

CONSTRUCTION

Cut dowel to size; drill a small hole at each end. Following the dimensions shown in the illustration, cut out the oval panel, slit as indicated, and insert dowel and glue to panel. Secure end points of dowel with tape. Cut out circular keel; slit an S-curve as shown. Pull panel through keel. Make a hole in each end of the dowel and fill with glue. Put nails through one hole in each button and insert the nails into dowel ends. Allow time for the glue to dry. Attach a 10-foot length of line to the button at each end of the dowel. Tie two ends together to form a bridle; add a tow ring.

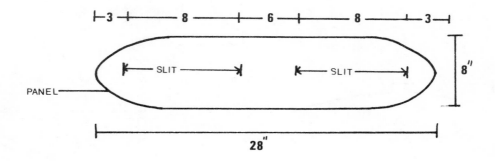

PARAFOIL

FRAME: none.

COVER: Ripstop nylon.
4 pieces, 6½ by 32 in.
4 pieces, 6½ by 35 in.
5 pieces, 33½ by 4½ in.
3 pieces, 13½ by 21 in.
3 pieces, 9 by 13 in.

LINE: 80–100 lb. test.

BRIDLE: 6 legs.

TAIL: drogue or long strip of nylon

WIND: 10–30 mph.

MATERIALS: scissors, pencil, ruler, needle and thread, grommets, tape, tow ring.

The parafoil was designed by Domina Jalbert. Based on the cross-section (airfoil) shape of an airplane wing, this kite is relatively easy to fly. Simply toss the parafoil into the air, allowing the cells to fill up with air. The kite will then rise upward.

CONSTRUCTION

Begin by cutting out three triangular shapes from the 9-by-13-inch pieces of fabric; these will be the front keels. Cut three triangular shapes from the 13½-by-21-inch pieces to form the back keels. Cut out five airfoil shapes from the 33½-by-4½-inch strips. Sew two of the triangular keels (one front, one back) to three of the airfoil shapes as shown. Note that the keels will overlap at some points; do not stitch the keels together. Sew top four panels (6½-by-32-inch pieces) to the top of the airfoils. Sew the bottom panels (6½-by-35-inch pieces) to the bottom of the airfoils. Place airfoils with attached keels at the ends and middle sections of the kite. Sew top section to bottom section at the back. The parafoil is completed. Simply punch in grommets and attach the bridle line with needle and thread to each keel, gather the six legs together, and attach a tow ring. Add the tail or drogue.

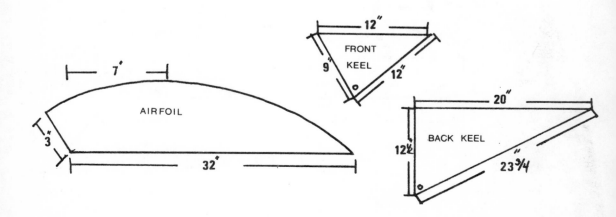

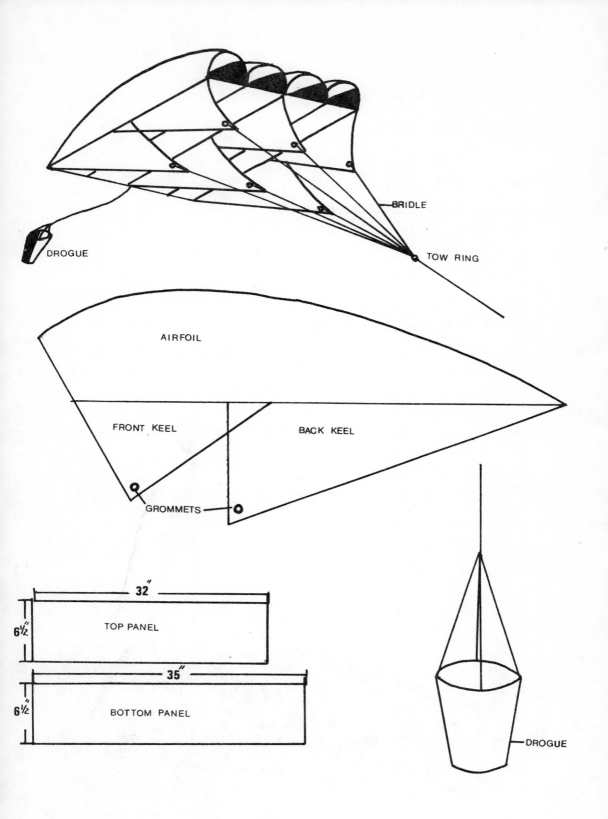

BRIDLE

DROGUE

TOW RING

AIRFOIL

FRONT KEEL

BACK KEEL

GROMMETS

32″

TOP PANEL

6½″

35″

BOTTOM PANEL

6½″

DROGUE

CARP WINDSOCK

FRAME: 1 rattan dowel, 30 by ¼ in.

COVER: cotton (2 pieces), 52 by 21 in.

LINE: 20 lb. test.

BRIDLE: 2 legs.

TAIL: none.

WIND: 5–30 mph.

MATERIALS: scissors, pencils, ruler, needle and thread, saw or utility knife.

Carp windsocks are flown as a custom on Boys' Day in Japan. These whimsical fish can be seen flying from boats or off porches. When you fly a steady kite, a carp windsock can be tied to the towline and raised right along with it.

CONSTRUCTION

Cut the two cover pieces into the shapes indicated in the illustration. Place them wrong sides together and stitch along sides, leaving mouth and tail ends open. Turn fabric right side out. Fold over one inch of fabric at the mouth of the carp to form hem. Stitch hem, leaving a space in which to push a dowel, bent into a circle, gently into opening. Once the dowel is completely in the hem, stitch the hem closed. Finish off the tail end by sewing a hem around the edge to prevent fraying. Don't stitch the tail end closed. Attach the bridle to points indicated in the illustration. The scales and eyes can be painted on with indelible ink. Note: When using marking pens, be sure to place a sheet of paper between the layers of fabric to prevent the design on one side from coming through to the other.

BRIDLE

TOW RING

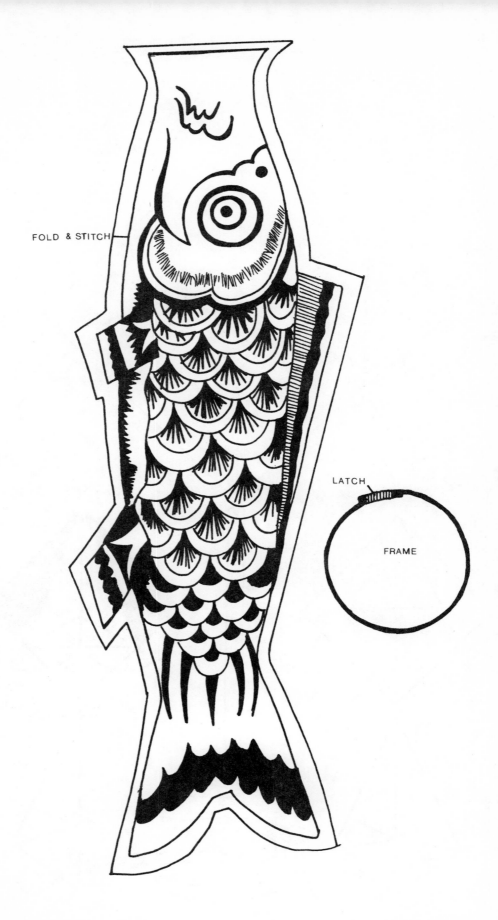

FOLD & STITCH

LATCH

FRAME

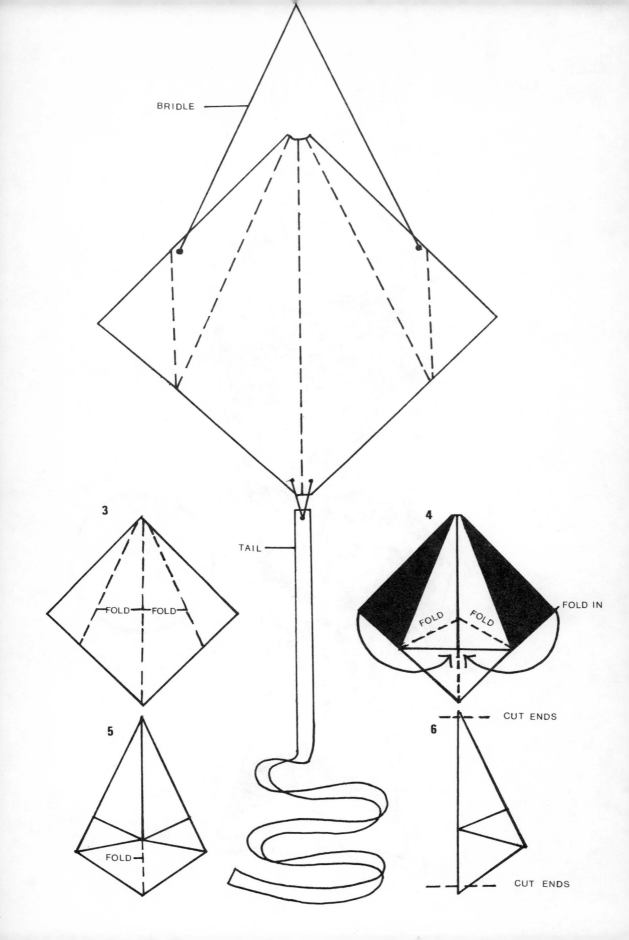

BRIDLE

TAIL

3

FOLD — FOLD

4

FOLD   FOLD

FOLD IN

CUT ENDS

5

FOLD

6

CUT ENDS

FLEXIKITE

FRAME: none.

COVER: 1 sheet of paper, 15 in. sq.

LINE: 10 lb. test.

BRIDLE: 2 legs.

TAIL: paper strip: 36 in.

WIND: 3–10 mph.

MATERIALS: scissors, pencil, ruler, paper, punch, tape.

This kite is very simple to make. Simply fold the paper, attach a bridle, and it is ready to go. I have made a flexikite from a lunch bag and flown it from sewing thread, thus turning a boring lunch hour into a kiteflying experience.

CONSTRUCTION
Cut paper to size. Following diagrams 1–6, folding the paper on the dotted lines. Follow step by step to #6. Cut off the tips. Tape and punch holes for bridle and tail. Attach the bridle and tail.

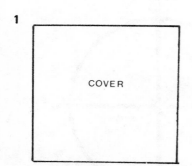

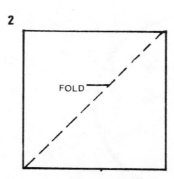

CENTIPEDE KITE

FRAME: 33 bamboo strips.
11, 32 by ⅛ by ¼ in.
22, 15 by ⅛ by ¼ in.

COVER: tissue paper or rice paper (11 sheets), 15 in. sq.

LINE: 20 lb. test.

BRIDLE: 2 legs.

TAIL: no tail, but streamers for side ornaments.

WIND: 5–15 mph.

MATERIALS: scissors, pencil, ruler, needle and thread, white glue, paint brushes, utility knife or saw.

The Chinese centipede kite was believed to frighten away all evil spirits from its flier. For this reason, the head disk was painted with a frightening face. Colorful feathers, dried wheat, or streamers can also be added to the sides of each disk for extra decoration.

CONSTRUCTION

Split and cut the bamboo strips to size. Take the twenty-two 15-inch strips, latch them together with string two at a time and glue to form eleven crosses. Bend, by soaking in hot water or heating over a candle, the remaining eleven strips to form circles and latch ends together with string and glue. Using a circular frame as an outline, trace out eleven circles on the paper; add one inch all around for hemming. Cut out covers. Attach crossed spars to circle frames by bracing (see p. 89). Nick edge of the cover papers and fold the edges over the frames; glue the covers to the frame. Attach disks to one another with string as shown in the illustration. Attach the bridle and side ornaments with needle and thread.

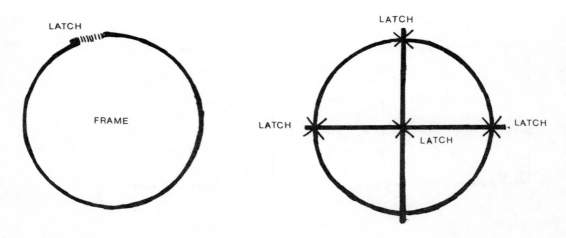

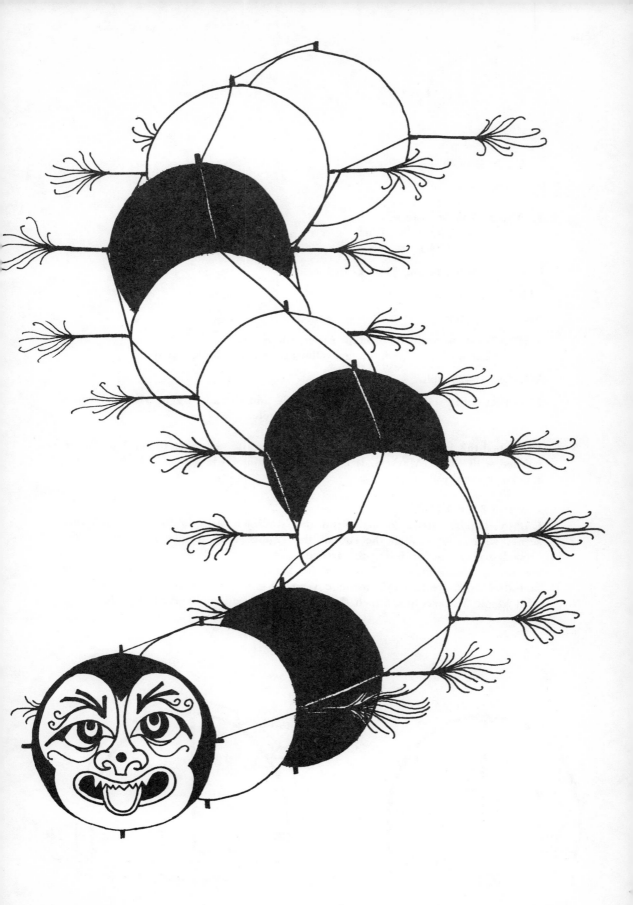

RAINBOW KITE

FRAME: 2 bamboo strips.
 31½ by ⅛ by ¼ in.
 12 by ⅛ by ¼ in.

COVER: white cotton, 14 by 17 in.

LINE: 20 lb. test.

BRIDLE: 2 legs.

TAIL: 14 strips of ribbon or crepe paper, 1 by 40 in.
 2 strips each of red, orange, yellow, green, blue, indigo, violet.

WIND: 10–25 mph.

MATERIALS: scissors, pencil, ruler, needle and thread, Magic Markers, white glue, tow ring, saw or utility knife.

I designed this kite based on the oriental octopus kite. The face of the kite can be painted with Magic Markers. It flies well in medium winds and looks quite spectacular in the sky.

CONSTRUCTION

Cut the bamboo strips to size. Bend the 31½-inch strip to form an arch and secure with string. Latch the end of the 12-inch strip to the mid-point of the arched spar, as shown. Using the arched frame as an outline, cut out cover material to fit, adding an inch all around for hemming. Glue the cover to the frame and attach the streamer tails to the cover with glue. Paint a rainbow on the cover with Magic Markers and attach the bridle with needle and thread. Add tow ring.

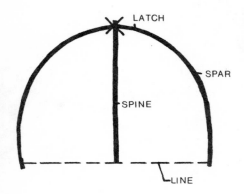

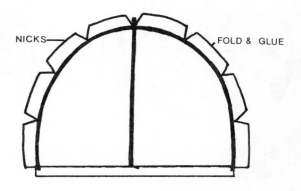

BRIDLE

TOW RING

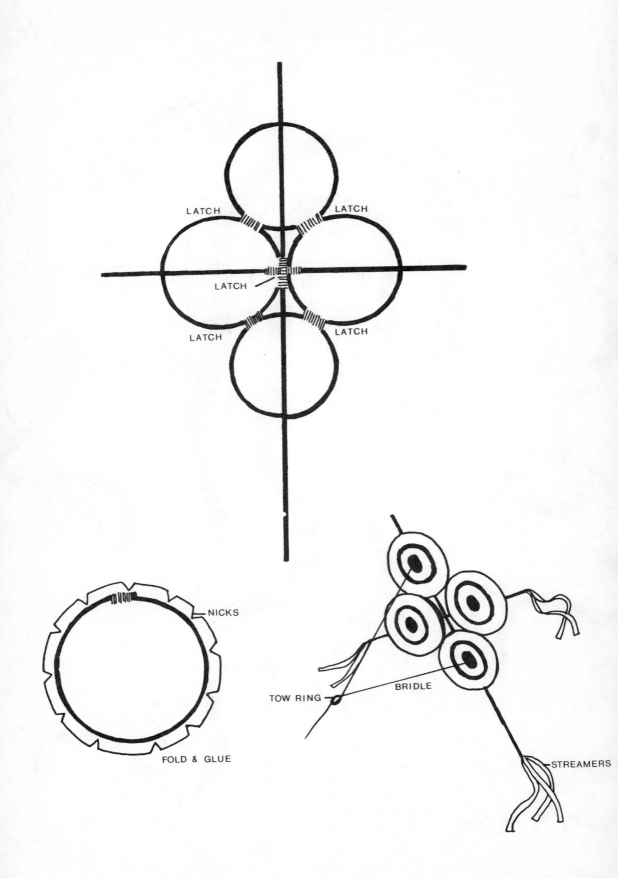

LATCH

LATCH

LATCH

LATCH

LATCH

NICKS

FOLD & GLUE

TOW RING

BRIDLE

STREAMERS

CHINESE DISK KITE

FRAME: 6 bamboo strips.
4, 29 by ⅛ by ¼ in.
1, 52 by ⅛ by ¼ in.
1, 24 by ⅛ by ¼ in.

COVER: tissue or rice paper (4 sheets), 12 in. sq.

LINE: 20 lb. test.

BRIDLE: 2 legs.

TAIL: streamers.

WIND: 5–7 mph.

MATERIALS: scissors, pencil, ruler, needle and thread, white glue, saw or utility knife.

This is one of many flat kites flown in China. It is a delicate kite that should be flown in light winds. The disks can be painted with bright colors so the kite will show up well in the sky.

CONSTRUCTION

Split and cut bamboo to size. Bend the four 29-inch strips, by heating over a candle or soaking in hot water, into circles. Latch ends together with string and glue. Attach the center of the 24-inch horizontal spar to the center of the 52-inch vertical spine with string and glue. Latch the circles to the crossed frame and each other at points indicated. Using a circle as an outline, cut out the covers, allowing an extra inch to hem and glue all around each circle. Nick the edges of the covers, fold, and glue them to the frame. Attach the bridle with needle and thread and paint with bright decorations. Add streamers for a tail.

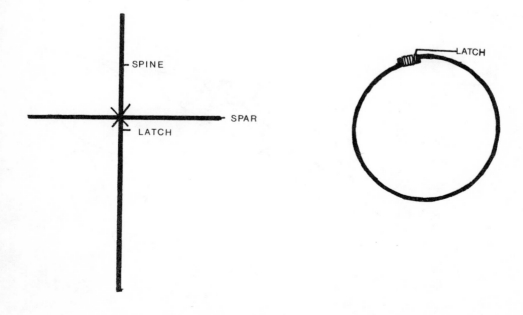

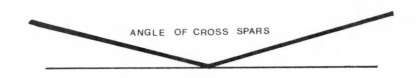

ANGLE OF CROSS SPARS

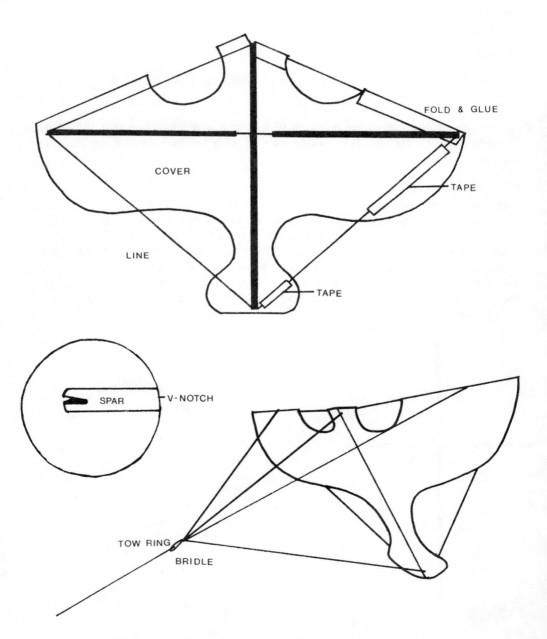

FOLD & GLUE

COVER

TAPE

LINE

TAPE

SPAR — V-NOTCH

TOW RING

BRIDLE

BRAZILIAN BIRD KITE

FRAME: 3 softwood dowels, 25 by ¼ in.

COVER: light cloth, 52 by 30 in.

LINE: 20 lb. test.

BRIDLE: 4 legs.

TAIL: none.

WIND: 5–20 mph.

MATERIALS: scissors, pencil, ruler, needle and thread, drill, metal saw file, nail
(1¼ in.), glue, cloth tape, saw or utility knife.

The Brazilian bird kite is an excellent flier and actually flutters its wing while
soaring through the sky. The traditional kite of Brazil, this bird is most maneuverable in medium winds.

CONSTRUCTION

Cut dowels to size. V-notch both ends of the spine and one end of the remaining
two spars. Drive a nail halfway through the spine, 6 inches from the top. Cut
off the head of the nail and file to a point. Drill small holes into the unnotched
ends of the remaining two spars about ½ inch deep. Secure the spars to spine by
fitting nail ends into the drilled holes. Run a line around the frame keeping it
taut. Cut the cover in the birdlike shape shown in illustration. Fold over the top
edge of the wing allowing string to move freely and glue or stitch in place. Following the diagram, tape the string to the lower flaps (of the bird's wings);
repeat with the flaps of the bird's tail. Attach the bridle with needle and thread.
Add tow ring.

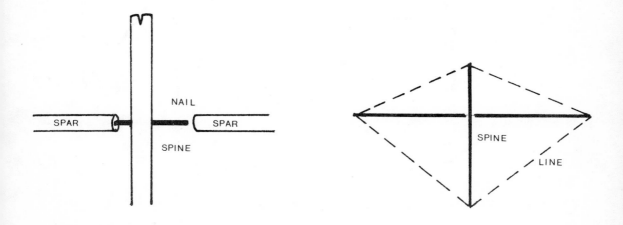

MUSICAL KITES

The ancient Chinese used musical kites as an early storm warning device. A farmer would fit his kite with a hummer and loft it into the night sky before retiring at the end of the day. The gentle wind would hum the entire household to sleep. If the sound became loud and irritating, it would awaken the farmer and his family, warning them of an approaching storm. The farmer then could take the necessary precautions to save his crops.

HUMMERS

A hummer can be made with a length of slender dowel and piano wire or a guitar string. Bend the dowel into a bow and tie the ends with the wire or string. Attach the bow to the back of your kite by placing loosely between cross bars and cover material. More than one hummer can be added for a more harmonious sound.

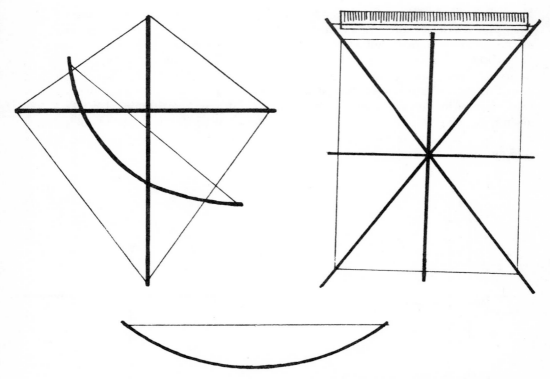

Left to right: Hummer, buzzer, harp, and pipe.

BUZZERS

To make your kite buzz, you will need a strip of paper and some glue. As shown in the illustration, wrap the strip of paper around a support string, spar, or spine and glue. Cut the paper into a fringe. This will create a buzzing sound when the wind vibrates against it.

HARPS

Stretch a few piano wires or guitar strings across the end of a box kite, without allowing them to touch one another. When the wind blows through the kite, the wires vibrate and produce an interesting harp sound.

PIPES AND FLUTES

Inexpensive plastic pipes or flutes can be fastened to the spars of a box kite, to produce another form of music.

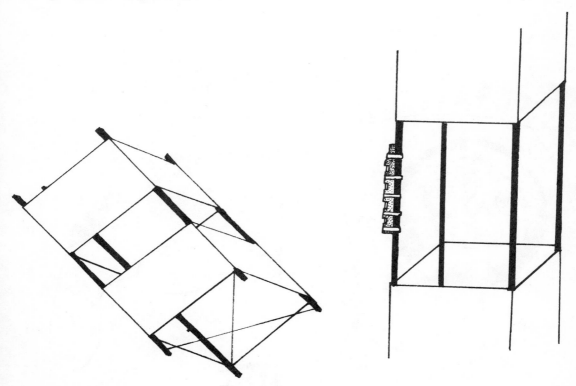

A CONSUMER'S GUIDE TO KITE BUYING

All of these kites are available at the wholesale sources listed on page 166.

PAPER KITES

If you have decided to buy a kite, remember the material and workmanship are critical to the kite's performance and versatility. While paper lends itself to a variety of shapes and sizes, it is the most fragile material used in kite making. When flying a paper kite, take care to fly it in light to medium winds of from one to seven miles an hour.

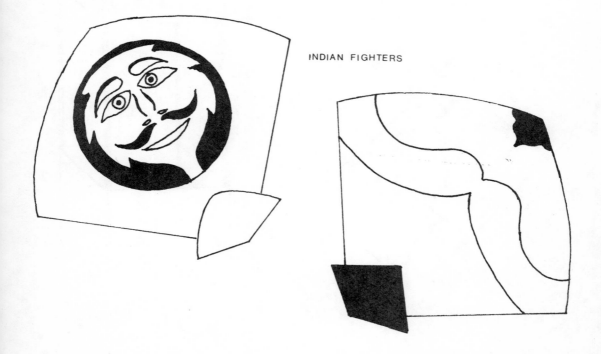

INDIAN FIGHTERS

INDIAN FIGHTER KITES

STANDARD FIGHTERS

These beautifully decorated kites are carefully balanced precision instruments. Still made in India by a handful of expert craftsmen, these kites require only the slightest breeze to send them soaring. However, some practice is required to keep them lofted. (If you are just beginning, I recommend the plastic Mylar version; it stands up well to the wear and tear of flying.) Available in many designs and colors, fighter kites make excellent wall hangings in their nonflying hours.

TUKKAL FIGHTERS

Basically fighter kites, these are another shape to choose from.

STAR OF INDIA FIGHTERS

These are round variations of the fighter kites and are flown in the same manner.

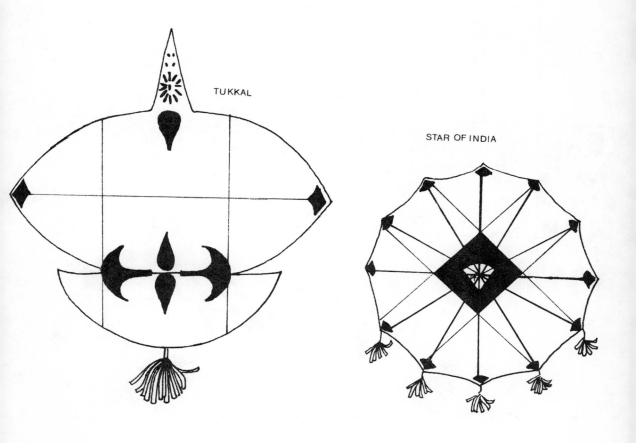

TUKKAL

STAR OF INDIA

THAI KITES

These colorful, flat kites, usually made of rice paper, are shaped like fish, birds, dragons, or turtles. Except for the long peacock and dragon kites, they are more decorative than flightworthy and some patience is required to get them aloft. Adding a tail will often help. They are fairly fragile and should be flown from a light line, in light to moderate winds.

PEACOCKS

These kites come with keels and ten-foot tails. Like the dragon kites, they are easy fliers and steady once lofted.

DRAGONS

The decorations of these kites generally portray cobras. Twenty-five feet long, these beauties are good fliers and wonderful to watch as they dance in the sky.

PEACOCK

FISH

TURTLE

COBRA DRAGON

OWL

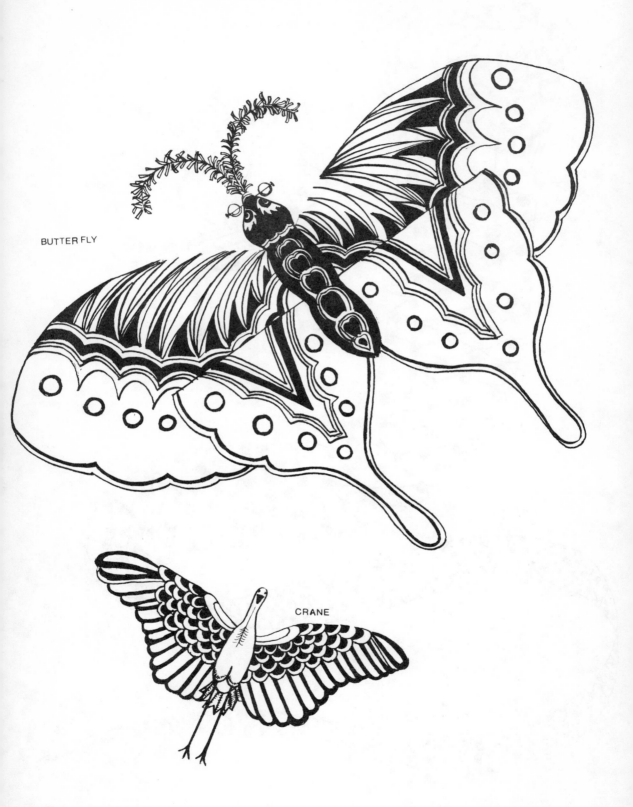

BUTTER FLY

CRANE

CHINESE KITES

China, the most likely birthplace of kites, has some of the most delightful paper kites made.

BUTTERFLIES

These delicate rice-paper kites are beautifully painted in bright colors. They fly in a light breeze and if you want, you can add tassel tails to dance behind them.

OTHER INSECTS AND BIRDS

Complete with three dimensional bodies, these whimsical creations are also available in silk. They are good fliers and lovely sights to behold. They come in the shape of dragonflies, crickets, and bees and cranes, blackbirds, magpies, swallows, and phoenixes. Closely related are kites shaped like centipedes and ferocious red bats.

BEE

JAPANESE KITES

BUTTERFLIES

These are colorful flat kites with pink streamer tails, but they are not the easiest kites to fly. A slight adjustment with the tail will make all the difference.

CENTIPEDES

This twelve-foot kite is made up of several circular disks, the first of which was designed with a scary face to ward off evil spirits from its flier. This is a difficult kite to fly, but it is possible to loft it with the right wind.

KABUKI CHARACTERS

The famed faces of Kabuki theater characters are the focal point of these hexagonal kites. These kites require a tail and should be flown in light winds.

CARP WINDSOCKS

These Japanese symbols of Boys' Day are available in various sizes and colors. Try flying one off the towline of another kite that is lofting steadily. Windsocks are not really kites and cannot fly on their own power.

KABUKI KITE

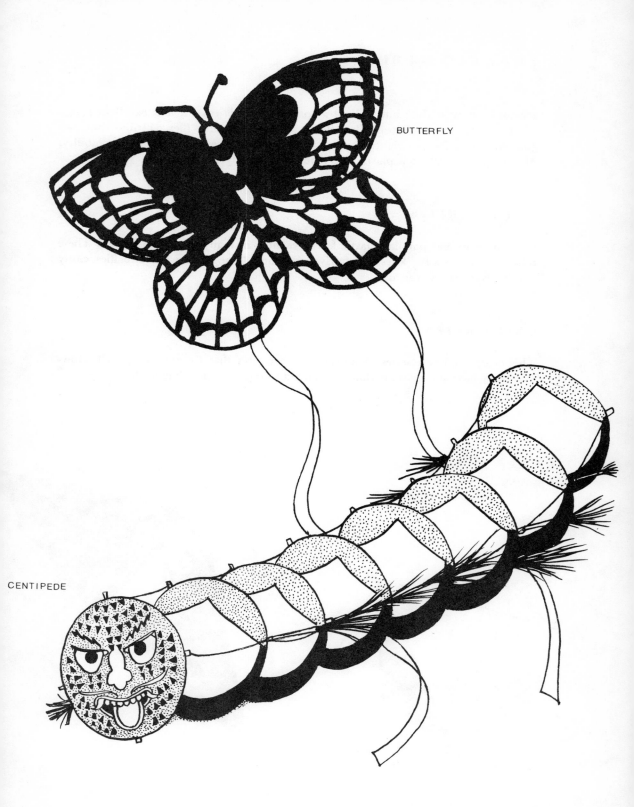

BUTTERFLY

CENTIPEDE

PLASTIC KITES

Plastic is stronger than but as light as paper. For this reason, it is excellent material to use for making kites. When flying a plastic kite, the flier will find that medium winds of four to eighteen miles per hour will give the best maneuverability. Mylar is a relatively new plastic that lends itself readily to kite designs.

HI-FLIER KITES

This company has popular plastic kites available in many shapes and styles. These relatively inexpensive kites are fairly good fliers. The delta-wing kite flies easily and holds its own in the air.

GAYLA KITES

This company has a series of inexpensive bat kites that fly extremely well. However, they have plastic spars that are difficult to replace when damaged.

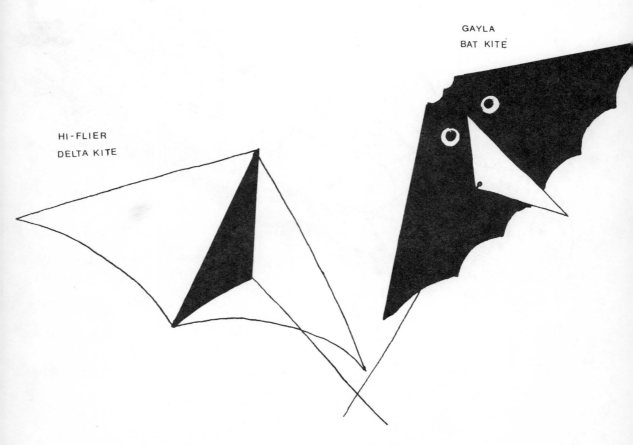

GAYLA
BAT KITE

HI-FLIER
DELTA KITE

GUNTHER KITES

Gunther, a toy manufacturer in West Germany, makes a line of sturdy plastic kites featuring brightly colored insects, dragons, and birds. Made of heavy plastic, they can be flown safely in winds of eight to fifteen miles per hour. These kites also feature spars made of wooden dowels that fit easily into plastic cups; they are also easy to replace if damaged. Gunther kites are available in better toy stores and kite shops.

GUNTHER KITES

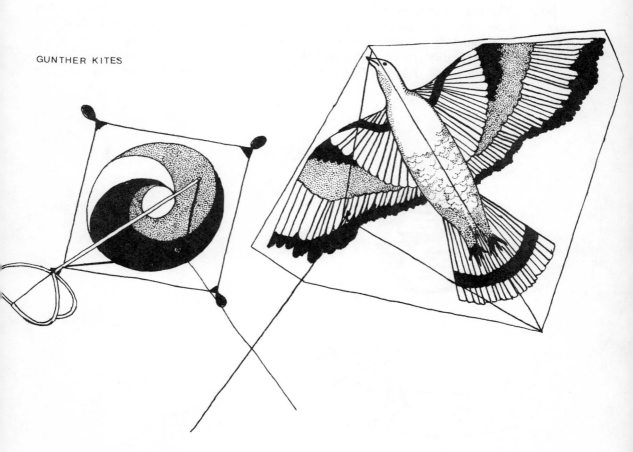

MYLAR DRAGONS

These kites, available in twenty-five- or fifty-foot lengths, are among the easiest kites to fly. Strong and flexible, they can be launched from your hand.

MYLAR FIGHTERS

Like their paper counterpart, these fighter kites require some skill to fly. However, they are much more durable than the paper variety and, for this reason, excellent for a beginner. They can withstand dips and nose dives without being destroyed. If the Mylar does tear, it can be easily repaired with Scotch tape.

MYLAR FLEXIKITES

These kites were designed by an aeronautics engineer and fly like birds. Because they are frameless, they can conform to almost any wind.

PETER POWELL STUNT KITES

The Peter Powell company has designed a new type of plastic kite. Basically flat kites with aluminum spine and spars, these kites are flown by double bridles. The fifty-foot tails are tubes that fill with air when the kites are flying. The kites are extraordinarily maneuverable and the flier can get the best results from them in medium winds. Whether flown singly or in tandem, they are quite a spectacle in the air.

MYLAR FIGHTER

MYLAR
DRAGON

CLOTH KITES

Cloth kites can be made of any fabric that is light and closely woven. Heavier than paper and plastic, cloth is also the strongest material used for making kites and can be flown in medium to strong winds of thirteen to thirty-one miles per hour.

BROOKITES

Brookites, from England, come in several models. Their cutter kite—a cloth diamond kite with a keel—available in a number of sizes, is well made and a superb flier in heavy winds. Brookites also feature a war kite (a Conyne design) that is brightly colored and an excellent flier.

BELGIAN KITES

A Belgian company makes a line of cloth kites based on a triangular-winged box kite. They are printed with graphics of eagles and butterflies. Their construction is on the heavy side, however, and they fly best in stronger winds.

ALAN-WHITNEY SPACE BIRDS

The Alan-Whitney Company makes these Ripstop nylon versions of the Conyne kite, or French military box kite. Brightly colored and sturdily constructed, these

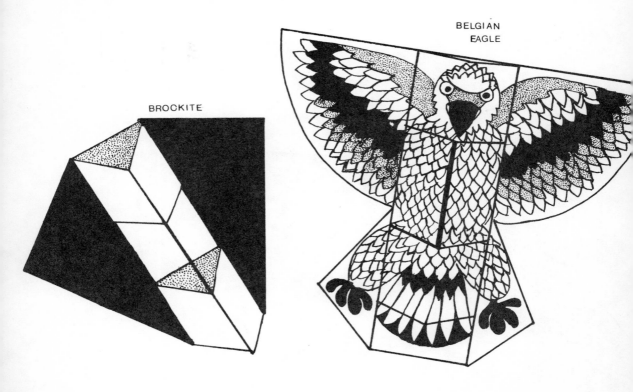

BROOKITE

BELGIAN
EAGLE

kites are excellent fliers. Available in two sizes the Space Birds fly stably in medium to strong winds.

WHITE BIRD KITES

White Bird kites, designed by Heloise Lockman and made in California, are not only works of art but also extremely good fliers. Each one is handmade and flawlessly constructed. One model, a diamond kite, has a bowed spine and a cover with an appliqué design. White Bird also makes dragon kites that feature rainbow tails. The faces of the dragons are appliquéd with sky signs such as moons, stars, clouds, etc., and are a sight to behold in the sky. I have stopped traffic with my rainbow dragon featuring a whale on the head, from a special Save-the-Whale selection.

PARAFOIL

The multicolored parafoil made by the Kite Factory is entirely of Ripstop nylon. It comes complete with its own drogue and folds into a convenient carrying case. This kite is a good buy and under normal circumstances will last forever.

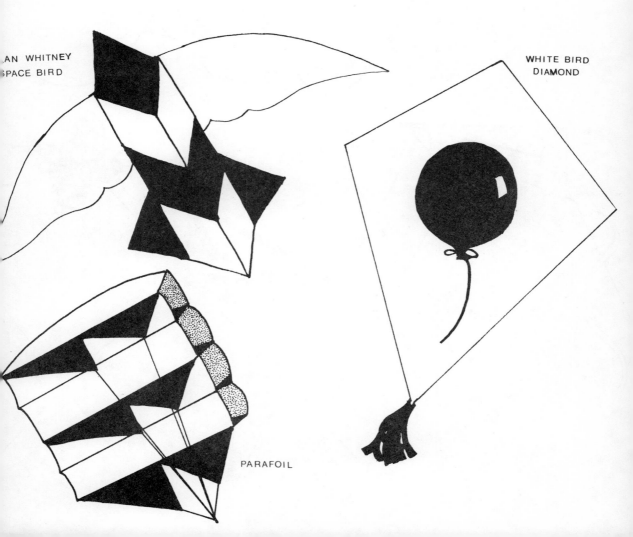

AN WHITNEY
SPACE BIRD

WHITE BIRD
DIAMOND

PARAFOIL

KITE FESTIVALS

ORGANIZING YOUR OWN KITE FESTIVAL

If you are considering starting a kite festival or contest, it would be to your advantage to encourage appropriate local organizations and clubs to sponsor your efforts in conjunction with their activities. For example, the Greater Boston Kite Festival is sponsored by the Committee for the Better Use of the Air. Not only will this kind of help get the idea off the ground, but it will also help generate public interest.

Here are a few ideas for prize-winning categories:

Homemade kites:
    a. largest
    b. smallest
    c. most decorative
    d. most unusual
    e. funniest

Bought kites:
    a. highest flier
    b. best controlled
    c. fastest launched
    d. best climber

All kites:
    a. Most kites flown on one line.
    b. Fighter kite outlasting all opponents.
    c. Highest altitude reached in a five-minute period.

PRIZES

Ribbons are usually given as prizes in kite festivals. However, check with local businessmen and see if they will donate prizes in exchange for publicity at the festival. If you have a local kite or hobby shop, be sure to encourage their involvement.

THE HIGHEST FLIER

An easy way to help the judges at the contest determine the highest flier is to begin with a time limit, have contestants stand at a starting line, and give a signal to begin. When the time limit is up, have the contestants, with the aid of a friend, walk the kites down. The winner is the flier with the longest string.

ANNUAL KITE FESTIVALS HELD IN THE UNITED STATES

ARIZONA
Encanto Park Festival
Encanto Park
Phoenix, Ariz.
    contact   Dave McDowell
                   Phoenix Parks Department
                   Phoenix, Ariz. 85007

CALIFORNIA
Carmel Kite Festival
Carmel Middle School
Carmel, Calif.
    contact   Carmel Lions Club
                   Carmel, Calif. 98621

Annual Celebrities Master Kite Tournament
Costa Mesa, Calif.
    contact   Optimists Club of Orange County
                   Allen Titmus
                   The Pecan Tree
                   840 Sonora Rd.
                   Costa Mesa, Calif. 92626

Annual Long Beach All-City Kites Festival
Long Beach, Calif.
   contact   Long Beach Parks and Recreation Department
               130 Cherry Ave.
               Long Beach, Calif. 90802

Let's Fly a Kite Festival
Marina Del Rey, Calif.
   contact   Gloria Lugo
               Let's Fly a Kite Shop
               Fisherman's Village
               13763 Fiji Way
               Marina Del Rey, Calif. 90291

Redondo Beach Kite Festival
   contact   Sunshine Kite Co.
               Redondo Beach Pier
               Redondo Beach, Calif. 90277

Ocean Beach Kite Festival
San Diego, Calif.
   contact   San Diego Parks Department
               San Diego, Calif. 92107

Ghirardelli Square Kite Flying Festival
San Francisco, Calif.
   contact   Come Fly a Kite, Inc.
               900 North Point
               Ghirardelli Sq.
               San Francisco, Calif. 94109

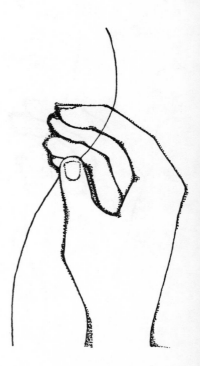

CONNECTICUT
Annual Bushnell Park Kite Day
West Hartford, Conn.
    contact   **The Greater Hartford Kite Society**
                Tim Wolf
                50 Castlewood Rd.
                West Hartford, Conn. 06107

DELAWARE
Great Delaware Kite Festival
Lewes, Del.
    contact   **Chamber of Commerce**
                P. O. Box 1
                Lewes, Del. 19958

DISTRICT OF COLUMBIA
Smithsonian Kite Contest
Washington, D.C.
    contact   **Smithsonian Residence Associates**
                Smithsonian Institution
                Washington, D.C. 20560

FLORIDA
Jacksonville Kite Festival
Jacksonville, Fla.
    contact   **Mayor's Office**
                Jacksonville, Fla. 32202

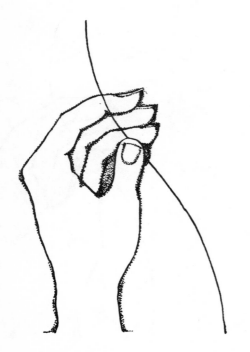
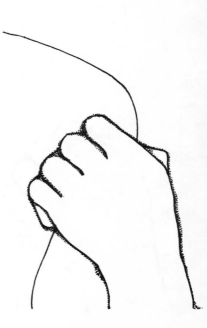

HAWAII
Oahu Kite Flying Festival
Honolulu, Hawaii
   contact   Honolulu Department of Parks and Recreation
               1201 Ala Moana Blvd.
               Honolulu, Hawaii 96841

IDAHO
Freeman Park Fly-In
Idaho Falls, Idaho
   contact   Idaho Falls Park and Recreation
               Box 220
               Idaho Falls, Idaho 83401

ILLINOIS
Prop Nutz Kite Fly
Chicago, Ill.
   contact   Prop Nutz Airplane Club
               Charles Sotich
               3851 West 62nd Pl.
               Chicago, Ill. 60290

MARYLAND
Maryland Kite Festival
Baltimore, Md.
   contact   Maryland Kite Society
               7106 Campfield Rd.
               Baltimore, Md. 21207

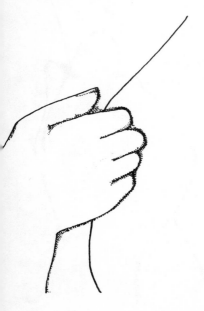
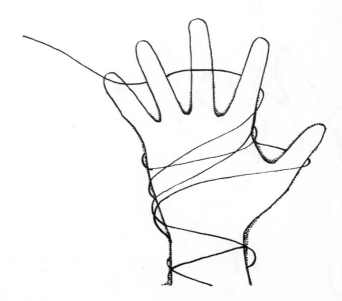

MASSACHUSETTS
The Greater Boston Kite Festival
Cambridge, Mass.
   contact   The Committee for Better Use of the Air
              23 Arrow St.
              Cambridge, Mass. 02138

Franklin Kite Festival
Franklin, Mass.
   contact   Cub Scout Park 29
              George Franklin
              465 Daily Dr.
              Franklin, Mass. 02038

NEW YORK
New York Kite Festival
New York, N.Y.
   contact   Go Fly a Kite
              1434 Third Avenue
              New York, N.Y. 10028

OHIO
Kite Day
Stow, Ohio
   contact   Silver Springs Park and Recreation Department
              Stow, Ohio 44224

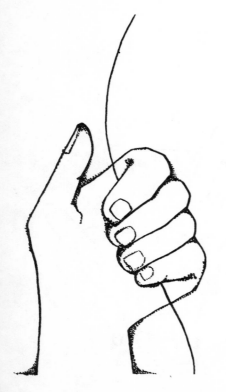

PENNSYLVANIA
Fly In and Design Contest
Indiana, Pa.
    contact   Lou Ann Gallanar
                The Smokehouse
                1128 Philadelphia St.
                Indiana, Pa. 15701

TEXAS
Bracken Ridge Kite Contest
San Antonio, Texas
    contact   Kite Radio and City Parks Department
                San Antonio, Texas 78212

VIRGINIA
Gunston Hall Kite Festival
Lorton, Va.
    contact   Louise Stockdale
                Gunston Hall Plantation
                Lorton, Va. 22079

WASHINGTON
Annual Kite Expedition
Seattle, Wash.
    contact   Pacific Science Center
                200 2nd Avenue
                Seattle, Wash. 98104

Seattle Center Kite Contest
Seattle, Wash.
    contact   Marty Dimock
                Seattle Center, Inc.
                Seattle, Wash. 98109

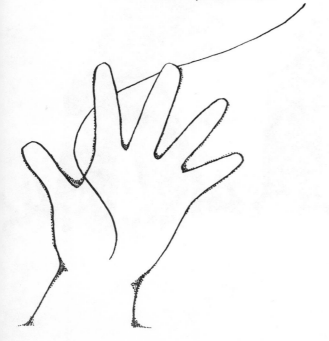
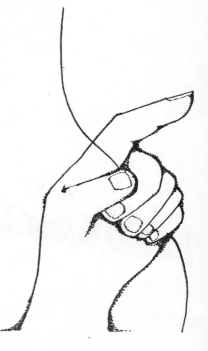

KITE CLUBS AND ORGANIZATIONS

One of the earliest kite clubs in the United States was formed in the 1880s in Terryville, Connecticut, next door to my own home town of Bristol. The ABCD Kite Club was founded by the Bunnell brothers, a couple of fun-loving guys, who, with a few friends, needed an excuse to go out and have a good time. Though the venture started out purely as a form of amusement, the club did have a hand in some early kite experiments. Their Sky-Scraper kite, a sixteen-by-twelve-foot, fifty-pound wonder, aided in a kite-towing escapade that created quite a stir among the locals and rated a mention in the Bristol Herald. On another occasion the group lofted a lit lamp into a night sky causing a few concerned neighbors to stare in wonderment toward heaven.

Fifty years before the founding of the ABCD Kite Club, a group of Philadelphia gentlemen started the Franklin Kite Club in 1835. The club was formed for the express purpose of continuing Ben Franklin's experiments with electricity. The club met once a week and members flew their cloth kites from copper wire, sometimes singly, sometimes in train. On one occasion during an electrical storm the group asked a passer-by to grab hold of a towline to test the kite's pull. The unsuspecting soul stood up in his cart with one foot on his horse for balance. He reached up and grabbed the towline. At that instant, a shock passed down the copper line through the man to the horse, causing quite a chain reaction. Luckily neither man nor beast were hurt.

One of the best-organized kite groups today is the American Kitefliers Association (AKA). Based in Baltimore, Maryland, the organization was founded by Robert Ingraham. Its membership is open to all those interested in flying and building kites for fun and recreation. The yearly dues are small and they entitle its members to a membership card and a year subscription to the quarterly magazine KITE LINES. For information write: AKA, 7106 Campfield Road, Baltimore, Maryland 21207.

The International Kitefliers Association (IKA), founded by famed kite expert Will Yolen, has a free membership open to any kiteflier who will supply a self-addressed stamped envelope. Its motto is "World-wide friendship through kite flying." Send to: IKA, 321 East Forty-eighth Street, New York, New York 10017.

KITE MANUFACTURERS AND SHOPS

MANUFACTURERS

Alan-Whitney Company, Inc.
P. O. Box 447
New Haven, Conn. 06502

Brookites, Ltd.
Francis Terrace, Junction Rd.
London N.19, England

The Kite Factory
678 West Prospect St.
Seattle, Wash. 98119

Nantucket Kite Man
P. O. Box 1356
Nantucket, Mass. 02554

Peter Powell Kites of America
1914 Sands Dr.
Annapolis, Md. 21401

Stratton Air Engineering
12821 Martha Ann Dr.
Los Alamitos, Calif. 90720

Synestructics Inc.
9559 Irondale Ave.
Chatsworth, Calif. 91311

SHOPS

Come Fly a Kite (distributor of White Bird kites)
900 North Point St.
Ghirardelli Sq.
San Francisco, Calif. 94109

High as a Kite
691 Bridge Way
Sausalito, Calif. 94965

Go Fly a Kite
1434 Third Ave.
New York, N.Y. 10028

Windy City Kites
1750 North Clark St.
Chicago, Ill. 60614

Rainbow Riders
36 Boylston St.
Cambridge, Mass. 02138

Rainbow Riders (summer)
Main St.
Hyannis, Mass. 02601

BIBLIOGRAPHY

Brummitt, Wyatt. KITES. New York: Golden Press, 1974.

Burkhart, Timothy. KITEFOLIO. Berkeley, Calif.: Ten Speed Press, 1974.

Dolan, Edward F., Jr. THE COMPLETE BEGINNER'S GUIDE TO MAKING AND FLYING KITES. Garden City, N.Y.: Doubleday, 1977.

Franklin, Benjamin. THE PAPERS OF BENJAMIN FRANKLIN. Vol. 4. Ed. L. W. Labaree et al. New Haven: Yale University Press, 1961.

Hart, Clive. KITES: AN HISTORICAL SURVEY. New York: Praeger, 1967.

Lloyd, Ambrose, et al. KITES: HOW TO FLY THEM, HOW TO BUILD THEM. New York: Holt, Rinehart and Winston, 1976.

Mouvier, Jean Paul. KITES. London: Collins, 1974.

Newman, Jay Hartley and Lee Scott. KITE CRAFT. New York: Crown (paperbound), 1964.

Pelham, David. THE PENGUIN BOOK OF KITES. New York: Penguin Books (paperbound), 1976.

Wagenvoord, James. FLYING KITES. New York: Macmillan (paperbound), 1969.

Yolen, Jane. WORLD ON A STRING. Cleveland: World Publishing, 1968.

Yolen, Will. THE COMPLETE BOOK OF KITES AND KITE FLYING. New York: Simon and Schuster, 1976.